A rant is a polemic, a forceful argument and in Scots "a noisy frolic". When Norman Finkelstein was told on the Today Programme that his book was "a bit of rant", he replied that all the great polemics such as Edmund Burke's *Reflections on the French Revolution*, Thomas Paine's *Rights of Man* and the *The Communist Manifesto* were rants, and his was just another. They are necessary voices in our national debate, but in this series we also like to keep in mind the gaiety and mischief of our noisy frolic. *Barking up the Right Tree* is a fine example.

Rant Six Rant Six Rant Six Rant Six Rant Six

Barking up the Right Tree

Paul Kavanagh

Vagabond Voices
Glasgow

First published in November 2015 by
Vagabond Voices Publishing Ltd.,
Glasgow,
Scotland.

ISBN 978-1-908251-59-6

Printed and bound in Poland

Cover design by Mark Mechan

Typeset by Park Productions

For further information on Vagabond Voices, see the website,
www.vagabondvoices.co.uk

In memory of Andy

Barking up the Right Tree

A brilliant budget if you're rich

So that was the budget. George Osborne, who looks more like a refugee from a low-rent Transylvanian castle with every passing day, promised that it wasn't going to be a giveaway budget as he stood outside Number 11 next to Danny Alexander, who looked like a man facing imminent execution, which he is. Danny knows that whatever goodies George has in his red box, there's nothing there that's going to save Danny's career or reputation.

Georgie was holding his red briefcase at arm's length like it contained the liver of a benefits claimant that he was going to have for lunch with a nice Chianti. There would be no bribes, no prezzies, no gimmicks, he said, except of course if you're a right-wing elderly Thatcherite who likes a swallie or three — so exactly the same voters that Jim Murphy is targeting then.

The collapse in oil prices means that inflation is lower than expected, which in turn means that interest payments on the eye-watering national debt are also less than predicted and also that the Treasury doesn't have to set aside so much dosh to cover inflation-related rises in benefits payments. Bad news for poor folk and bad news for Scotland's oil industry, but at least the constant reminders from Unionists that Scotland is too poor have given the orifice into which Danny Alexander has inserted himself an extra £6 billion to play with in bribes, which he can give away to potential Murphoid voters — most of whom live in the richest parts of the country. Sorry, not bribes, incentives for hard-working families and people who inherit loads of money from mummy and daddy. So that terribly clever and wise Gordie Broon was right then: this is UK redistribution and pooling resources in action. You pool, and people better off than you get a share.

Anyway, George was feeling very pleased with himself because he's worked terribly hard to reduce the national debt and now has got it down to a mere £1.5 trillion, most of which goes to pay bankers' bonuses and pay rises for company directors. He's also going to implement some policy wonkishness to reform inheritance tax — which is code for giving tax breaks to people who are already rich enough that they really don't need any tax breaks. Oh and he promised another £45 billion in cuts still to come, but the people who benefit from the inheritance tax changes are unlikely to notice, or indeed care. Who worries about austerity when you've got a nice pile to look forward to from the bank of mum and dad? Or even the bank of distant auntie that you're barely on speaking terms with?

There was a wee sop for drinkers and motorists. Beer duty got cut by a penny, so if you drink a couple of hundred pints you'll get a free one, which will enamour you so much with George's budget that you'll vote Tory. Or at least that's the theory. In practice you'll be too plastered to tell the difference between George Osborne and a big steaming pile of rancid pork, although to be fair that's a tough call at the best of times.

Motorists also got a promise that petrol duty won't be raised this year, pleasing the Jeremy Clarksons of this world no end. There was bugger all for you in this budget if you rely on public transport, but then George is of the school that holds that if you need to take a bus instead of a chauffeured limo then you're probably a benefits claimant and your JSA should be sanctioned.

Wee Danny Alexander's big hope for saving his skin came with an announcement of a plan for a new offence of "corporate failure to prevent economic crime." It's far too little too late, and Danny knows that if the measure was ever seriously introduced it would see the entire coalition cabinet and their Labour predecessors in jail, because collectively and corporately they embarked on a policy of allowing the banks and the financial companies to do pretty much what they liked, leading to financial armageddon and constant newspaper headlines telling us it's all the fault of poor people, benefits claimants, Scots and whoever it is that the *Daily Mail* has it in for this week.

In a bizarre historical exegesis, George also went on a bit about the Battle of Agincourt. That's modern Conservatism for you, but UKIP voters in Essex like that sort of thing, even though most of them think that Agincourt is a nightclub in Magaluf. George is going to spend a million quid to celebrate the English beating the French and their Scottish allies way back in 1415, not that he's bitter or anything. Actually there is no historic record of Scotland aiding the French at the battle of Agincourt, as we were in the huff with them at the time due to the refusal of the French to recognise bridies as a foodstuff. But it allowed George to have his little gloat, and that's all that matters. It's a gloat that can easily be paid for by sanctioning the Jobseeker's Allowance of about three thousand claimants. Pooling and sharing, thanks Gordie.

And you were fed up because they kept harping on about bleedin' 1966. In the year 2566 a rump UK government — if Westminster hasn't sunk beneath the waves by then due to rising sea levels — will be spending 100 quintillion quid (inflation adjusted) to celebrate Bobby Moore and remind everyone that Scotland has a rubbish football team. The Tory chancellor of the day will pay for it by sponsored kitten drownings and pulling the wings off flies. At least Scotland will be independent by then so we won't be paying for it.

The most significant announcement was the unveiling of a new design for the pound coin because the old one is always being faked. Which by a fitting coincidence is exactly like compassionate Conservatism. Mind you, asking George to fake compassion is a bit like expecting Vlad the Impaler to do an impression of a cosmetic surgeon, and in Scotland at least, the Tories will still be skewered.

19 March 2015

Devolution Jenga and the wowsie vowsie

Once upon a time there was a vow. It was not just any common or garden vow, oh no, it was super-duper, cast in iron, and guaranteed by the word of Gord. It was a wowsie vowsie, a holy and sacred thing. A couple of days before the referendum Jackie Bird told us, not once but repeatedly, on BBC Reporting LabourScotland that we were being vowed devo max. Was it not devo max times ten? Was it not devo max with sugary sprinkles? Jackie asked. The Lord Gord, who she was interviewing at the time, looked down from his cloud and nodded sagely. It was going to be the closest thing to full-on federalism possible, like page three but with the nipples discreetly hidden in a sexy and coquettish pose. And to be fair, that sort of thing is very difficult for Gordie to pull off, although he does have the pout off pat.

Well I say that Jackie was interviewing the Gordie, but it was an interview in the same sense that a fanzine writer interviews the object of his or her late-night fantasies just before scribbling a story that gets published on a specialist website whose readers usually don Spock ears before accessing it. And because fantasy is infectious, Davie Cameron even indulged Gordie in the fantasy that he was still prime minister and actually had some power to do the things he promised. Flush as he was with the mighty power of self-delusion, Jackie cooed and oohed as Gordie vowed to give Scotland the earth, the moon, the asteroids and everything in the solar system except the gas giants. And they were only omitted because they already have seats in the House of Lords.

Getting into his stride, because there's nothing a galactic ego loves more than unquestioning reverence — except possibly the black hole at their centre — Gordie swore blind that he'd personally torture the leaders of the three main parties by forcing them to watch reruns of indoor bowling from Coatbridge presented by Dougie Donnelly until they complied and delivered home rule. Scotland was going to get absolutely everything except its paws on the TV remote control, so Jackie's BBC bosses' jobs were safe. And just so there could be no doubt, there was going to be a very special edition of a tabloid newspaper, with faux parchment writing and everything. Jackie nearly fainted. Oh Gord.

Voters in Scotland can remember all this clearly, because the great majority of us were not sniffing glue at the time, and were fully aware that the hallucinations were not ours.

And so it came to pass. There was a No vote, and the vowsie began to leak air more rapidly than a balloon that's been burst by a pin and is hurtling across the room as quickly as a Labour MP in search of an invoice which can be claimed on expenses. Never has a reputation plummeted so far and so fast since Rolf Harris was arrested.

First came the Smith Commission, which

proceeded to fillet the vowsie with every phone call from Labour, Tory and Lib Dem HQs in London. The vowsie was bayoneted by the MoD, sanctioned by the Department for Work and Pensions, and sworn at by uncivil servants. Oh no, they chorused, that vowsie will never do. You can't do that, you can't put the interests of Scotland above the interests of a Whitehall mandarin; it's just not British. So the Unionist parties turned the Smith Commission negotiations into a game of devolution Jenga, each one trying to remove as much as possible without toppling the entire edifice, hollowing it out and neutering it in the grand British tradition of screwing the voters behind their backs. It's what we voted No for.

And then, finally, the report was published. Scotland reacted with the same resigned apathy it displayed during the Royal Wedding, although with relief that this time we didn't have Nicholas bloody Witchell on the telly twenty-four bleedin' hours a day telling us to rejoice. Scotland was to get some unusable tax powers, a tangerine in its stocking at Christmas, control of road signs, and Westminster would make a pinkie promise that it wouldn't ever abolish Holyrood. The reality of course being that if it ever tried, Scotland would become independent quicker than you could say, "You know where you can stick your sovereignty of the Crown in parliament, pal."

The Smith report disappeared into the maws of Westminster committee rooms, which then managed to prove that it is in fact possible to gut something that has already been flayed, defleshed and boiled until nothing is left but bone. Westminster, the MPs and Lords opined, couldn't possibly give a guarantee that Holyrood could never be abolished, what with the absolute sovereignty of the Westminster parliament and everything. And wasn't it terribly unfair that Scotland was to get a tangerine when England, Wales and especially Northern Ireland had their own citrus-based demands as well? Scotland can't possibly get control of road signs, because the format of road signs on the A9 near Inverness must be discussed in detail in a planning meeting in Leighton Buzzard public library. People in Clacton and Croydon have deeply held views about the spelling of the Gaelic language version of "Give Way". Scotland must give way to the control freaks of Westminster, again.

The public must be consulted, said the MPs and Lords, who have previously shown little inclination to consult the public on anything much. And Westminster must debate and cogitate on whether these proposals should be introduced at all. Meanwhile Gordie the guarantor was nowhere to be seen, vanishing from public view along with Alistair as their party's influence on Scottish public life evaporated like a Labour Party listening exercise.

All over Scotland there is a growing rumbling of muttered voices as Yes voters say to No voters, "Told you so," and No voters reply, "Oh shut up, don't rub it in." And a determination grows that if Westminster politicians won't deliver on their promises, then Scotland will replace them with politicians who will actually represent what the country wants. The only thing Gordie has guaranteed is his party's destruction.

26 March 2015

Here comes Gordie to save Magrit

In a secret location in Parkhead in the East End of Glasgow, in front of a packed crowd of a dozen Labour employees bussed in from party headquarters, some people invited from the press, and the last remaining member of the Glasgow East Labour constituency party who isn't Magrit Curran or one of her relatives, Gordie Broon came to save the Labour Party. Again. You can tell two things whenever the Labour Party trots out Gordie. Firstly, there's a vote in the offing, and secondly, polling shows they're going to lose it unless they make promises they have no intention or ability to keep. It's the official start of the election campaign, and Labour's in deep deep doo-doo. Hence the Gordathon.

Once upon a time, Labour could call a public meeting in the East End and thousands of punters would come out on a cold March morning to attend. They'd wave and cheer. There would be bunting. Gordie's secret behind closed doors invitation only meeting is the closest Labour dares get to a public meeting in the East End these days. This is on account of the fact that when Labour allows members of the actual East End public to get close to their elected representatives, the East End public expresses incredulity at Labour's policies using phrases that start with "get ye tae ..." and ending, for the politer ones at least, with words like "ya muppet".

When the SNP pull stunts like this involving Alicsammin, they get asked why Alicsammin is speaking for the party and not Nicla, and wondering is done about who is pulling whose strings. No one accuses Gordie of pulling any strings, because there are no strings long enough to reach from planet Earth to wherever it is that Gordie lives. When Labour do it, it's just Gordie being a respected elder statesman who has the immense advantage of not being Jim Murphy. This is of course not the only difference: for one thing, people actually like Nicla. However, a more salient difference is the fact that the SNP do actually invite members of the public to public meetings, and can do so safe in the knowledge that the public will not spend the duration of the meeting yelling "Burn the witch!" and enquiring whether any retail outlets at the Parkhead Forge have special buy-one-get-one-free offers on pitchforks, tar and feathers.

Gordie was here to remind us benighted East End folk that he's a big hitter who's going to hit big things. That is when he can be bothered to divert his attention from his speaking career and thon vow he was supposed to be guaranteeing. Mostly the big thing he hits is the fee he charges for public speaking. He'll be hitting that big now that he's officially retiring, as opposed to unofficially just not turning up to do the job he's paid for.

Gordie took the obligatory swipe at the SNP. They're in cahoots with the Tories and he's got the paperwork to prove it. So there. It was leaked to him by some obliging civil servant at the Treasury, so it must be true and completely above board. The SNP has signed up to Tory austerity, said Gordie. Just like Ed Balls, he didn't add. Only one of those propositions is not really true, and it's not the one about Ed Balls.

This time, when he wasn't attacking the SNP, Gordie came to make another vow. Or in this instance a pledge, presumably because it's shinier and has a nicer polish. Gordie's pledge has yet to be tarnished by reality. He's going to guarantee that if Labour get into power there will be an extra £800 million for the Scottish budget which they can spend on nurses and bandages and finding jobs for all the Labour MPs who are going to be made redundant. The NHS is of course a devolved matter, and it makes no difference how many Labour Westminster MPs we vote for: Holyrood still has the final say. Labour is hoping we haven't noticed. Perhaps it's just slipped Gordie's mind, like guaranteeing the Vow. Easily done. After all, he's forgotten and Labour have forgotten that Gordie is a retiring backbench MP who has no power to pledge anything at all. They're hoping we haven't noticed that either, blinded as we are by Gordie's polish.

Mind you, just the other week Jim Murphy, the nominal leader of the Labour accounting unit, was promising there was going to be £1 billion in extra funds for the Scottish budget, so already £200 million have gone missing. The new pledge is devaluing even more quickly than the Vow did. Possibly the missing £200 million has gone on expenses. Labour MPs are high-maintenance.

There's going to be a lot more of this over the next month. But it won't make any difference. Magrit's still toast. Just ask the real East Enders, the people Labour hasn't been listening to for the past few decades, the people who don't get invited to Labour's public meetings in their own community. And that's precisely why Labour is in so much trouble.

Five weeks and counting Magrit. Then it will the East End's turn not to invite you.

31 March 2015

Jim keeps trotting out the same old lies

Labour has been sending out election leaflets — in the post because they can't persuade any volunteer activists to do it for them. Just the other day another popped through the letter box, courtesy of an over-burdened and underpaid privatised postal service worker, telling us that we need to stop the Tories from being the largest party because another Tory government would be a disaster for Scottish families. Like those families who work for the privatised postal service that Labour has no intention of un-privatising, who will see their disaster continuing unchecked.

The claim that Labour needs to be the largest party is constantly repeated by Jim Murphy and his dwindling band of minions, the haemurphoids — they're reddish, irritating and dangle from a bum. As claims go, it's not actually true: Labour doesn't need to be the largest party, that's not how the House of Commons works, and you'd think that the Labour Party ought to know this. But then they've not been paying attention to Scotland for the past twenty years, we shouldn't really expect them to have been paying attention to anything much else either. Except their expenses claims of course. The truth is that the government is formed by the party that can get its budget and Queen's Speech through the voting lobby, and that could just as easily be the second largest party with the tacit support of the third largest.

Jim himself acknowledges that it's not true, speaking in that creepily quiet exasperated tone he adopts whenever it is pointed out to him that he is, in fact, talking a load of cack again. He was at it again being interviewed by Jim Naughtie on Radio 4 on Wednesday, and even the Naughtie one, who once referred to the Labour Party as "we", seemed to be getting exasperated. Press the Murphy Jim on the issue and he'll state that the last time the second largest party formed the government was in 1924, so Jim does actually admit that he's been talking cack.

A great many things have changed since 1924, for starters in 1924 the Labour Party was actually socialist and would have dealt with a suppose-he's-Tory like Jim quicker than a person with a bad case of piles would have reached for a suppository. But what's not changed is arithmetic.

If the second largest party and the third largest party together can form a majority in the Commons, the largest party still isn't going to form the government. Numbers haven't changed since 1924, and neither has the way the Commons calculates a majority. Jim knows that. He even admits it. He's just hoping that the second largest party forming the government doesn't happen very often, and that the last time it happened being ninety years ago means voters will think it's as implausible as a lottery win, or indeed as implausible as Labour ever returning to its socialist roots. But it looks likely to happen this year, which is great news for Scotland, and dreadful news for Jim. The electorate of Scotland have discovered the Preparation H that's going to soothe the irritation of a right-wing Labour Party. And Jim's shrinking.

In the same interview Jim accused the SNP of "overflowing with arrogance". He'd know a lot about arrogance. Labour in Scotland has traded on nothing else for the past thirty years. Jim's about to discover what the rest of us think of his party's arrogance, hence his growing hysteria.

Meanwhile, in an effort to clench Labour's flabby buttocks really tightly, Shadow Chancellor Ed Baws has come to Scotland to warn us that a vote for the SNP is a vote for the Tories and a vote for austerity. That's the Ed Baws who said that he wouldn't undo any of George Osborne's recent budget. Ed wants Labour to win so he can present his own budget which will be remarkably similar to Osborne's. And then Ed will get to stand outside Number 11 Downing Street waving his bright red Baws bag full of austerity policies with a Labour sad face. Only Ed won't be looking very sad, since he's only got one look and that's smug and self-satisfied. The only people who won't be remotely satisfied with an Ed Baws budget are traditional Labour voters.

Sadly for Ed and his smugness and his shadow Baws bag however, the visit to Scotland to scare the natives was overshadowed by the news that over one hundred business leaders have written to the *Daily Telegraph* to warn that if Labour gets into power then that rogue planet that was predicted by the Mayan calendar will come hurtling through space and wreak havoc on all parts of the UK that are not owned by non-doms and bring about the end of civilisation as we know it — at least in non-Tory voting areas where business leaders think it would be hard to tell the difference. And some of the business leaders had their names printed in a big purple font, so it's extra serious. Perhaps those who didn't get their names in big purple font were only predicting the slaughter of the firstborn and a rain of frogs, and not the full suite of Mayan plagues.

Labour's trying to laugh off the letter as just a wee joke for April Fool's Day, what with business persons being a natural Tory constituency who are going to support the party that's going to let them away with paying less tax. Secretly however, Labour is pretty annoyed, since their record in government of letting businesses off paying tax is every bit as reprehensible as the Tories'. Haemurphoids issued statements saying that the letter should be ignored because it had of course been orchestrated by the Tories and was therefore, by definition, a lie.

This is all very different from last year during the referendum campaign when Labour was telling Scotland to take as the holy writ of the Lord Gord the direst warnings of leading business executives and Michelle the Moan that voting in a way they didn't like would bring about economic destruction and ruin, and we should all cower in fear of the wrath of Duncan Bannatyne. Last year, Labour clapped and cheered when business leaders issued dire predictions of the end of the universe after being put up to it by the Tories. But we're in a different election now, and now we know that according to Labour hysterical warnings of the end of civilisation are only true when they refer to Scotland. Glad that's been cleared up then.

The voters will be clearing up a lot of things on 7 May, starting with the Labour Party in Scotland. Poor Labour, karma's come and bit them on the haemurphoids.

2 April 2015

Alistair Carmichael and the creepy janitor from Scooby-Doo

Poor Alistair Koalamichael. There he was sitting in his tree, chewing eucalyptus leaves in the hope it would cover the smell of a plot gone wrong even though the stench floors listeners with his every breath, and now the scandal has backfired on him. That's what happens when you try to weave a tangled web with those chubby koala fingers.

The last Lib Dem Secretary of State for Scotland has promised an enquiry which conveniently won't report back until sometime after the next election, by which time, such is the public anger at a blatantly transparent smear attempt from the Scottish Office, there are likely to be no Tory, Labour or Lib Dem MPs north of Carlisle and no one will care anyway. These things happen Alistair, karma kills Carmichael.

The Scotland Office is supposed to be Scotland's voice in the UK government, yet under the last Labour government it became the propaganda wing of Unionism in Scotland. That was Jim Murphy's legacy; Alistair is just continuing in the same cack-handed tradition. The purpose of the Scotland Office is to smear opponents of the Union. It's a tax funded version of the Tory press.

As smears go it was never one likely to have much

traction. If Alistair had been possessed of as many brain cells as there are Lib Dem MPs, he might have realised that the constantly repeated trope that the SNP "really want the Tories to win because it gives them a better chance of winning another referendum" is only true like the theory that the moon landings were really filmed in the Beechgrove Garden is true, or it's true that Westminster enquiries always produce answers that satisfy everyone just like the ending to an episode of Scooby-Doo. It's one of those truthy things that's only believed by those who have a vested interest in believing it.

The real truth, as opposed to the truthiness that Labour and the Lib Dems cling to like a burst life jacket in the middle of a Scottish storm, is that the SNP don't want a Tory government. We had a Tory government during the last referendum campaign, a wee fact that the victors have clearly forgotten. A Tory government is not what anyone in Scotland wants, except the half-dozen people who voted for Ruth Davidson and David Mundell.

The person responsible for the leak that aimed to dry up the Scottish tsunami is already known to Alistair. Of course, if Alistair already knows who leaked the memo, then why is there any need for a long and convoluted enquiry that won't report back for weeks? Since the person responsible is already known, then surely the enquiry will consist of Alistair pointing his chubby koala finger at the miscreant, who will then say "I'd have got away with it if it wasn't for those pesky kids," and the entire enquiry will be over and done with quicker than an episode of

Scooby-Doo. No need for the Mystery Machine and running down corridors saying "Zoinks!" Although come to think of it, Alistair does bear a suspicious resemblance to the creepy janitor wearing a rubber face mask.

And there was me thinking that cartoon politics was the preserve of Jim Murphy, BA Politics (failed), doing his Wile E. Coyote impression, running off a cliff while borne aloft on nothing more than John McTernan's frantic spinning and the dust created by a thousand press releases.

That's what neither Alistair nor Jim gets. The electorate of Scotland are grown-ups, one of the most sophisticated and aware electorates in the world. We can see right through them and their infantile tricks, and we're sick to the back teeth of the childish and childlike approach to politics which characterises this government and the Labour Party. Then they complain because we don't take them seriously. These things happen eh.

7 April 2015

Labour are tainted by Tony's kiss of death

The traditional image of death is a black cowled skeleton carrying a scythe; in the case of the Labour Party it's orange skinned with tombstone teeth, and it carries a consultancy contract with a Central Asian dictator when it's not justifying Israeli bombing campaigns in Gaza. Now he whose name must not be mentioned has intervened in the election campaign to give Ed Miliband his full support.

Someone must have said his name three times out loud while turning anticlockwise, and now Ed Miliband has received the endorsement of death. Ed's tried not to notice, just in case anyone reminds him that Ed Balls used to be a Tory too. But it's not all unremittingly negative: Tony Blair is still quite a bit more left wing than Jim Murphy, and as a bonus he also has less incontinent eyebrows and his eyes aren't quite so staringly mad.

Tony warned against the dangers of Scottish independence. Escaping the clutches of the likes of Tony would be bad for Scotland because we'd no longer have him to put in a good word for us with Central Asian dictators. And the price of oil is dropping so Tony thinks independence is a no-no, although he was still opposed last year when oil was riding high. Clearly the price of oil is as relevant as the price of a bag of sugar. The Unionists do keep going on about the plummeting price of oil, however, the logical corollary is that there must be a price per barrel at which independence becomes a moral and economic necessity. Perhaps they should tell us what price that is then? Don't go holding your petrol pump for an answer.

But it's not really about Scotland. Tony was far more concerned that Scottish independence would have relegated Britain from the premier league of nations. The UK needs Scotland's resources so it can keep playing keepie-uppie with the Americans. And now we know where Jim Murphy gets his love of fitba references from. He learned everything he knows on the knee of Tony Blair, playing with balls.

No one in the modern Labour Party likes to mention Tony Blair, not even Jim, although they'll bring up every other figure from Labour's past — with the possible exception of Neil Kinnock. Aneurin Bevan, Harold Wilson, John Smith, they all get dragged out from time to time to lend some credibility to a party that's as plausible as a black moustache on an audience member at a political debate. But not the Tory Blair, he's too close to the fake moustache truth of modern Labour, the black evil smear on Labour's lying lips.

Tony Blair, let us not forget — even though Labour would like us to — was by far the most successful leader Labour's ever had. Tony took the party to three election victories in a row and won large absolute majorities every time. He did it by sacrificing the chickens of his spineless backbenchers on the altar of the Satans of the City.

When Labour got into power in 1997 after the long dark decade and a half of Tory rule, that seemingly endless winter of the soul and hibernation of hope, Tony had a majority of 179 seats. We celebrated, we rejoiced. Spring had arrived and hope could flourish. Change was in the air. In 2001 he won with a majority of 167. Tony had the power to do anything that Labour wanted, the entire British state lay prostrate at the party's feet, the Labour Party had delivered the working classes and huddled masses to the promised land. But the British Parliamentary Road to Socialism ended in a missile blast on the way to Baghdad and Labour died with it. Hope died too, crushed in the rubble.

Back in 1997 we were still doe-eyed and hopeful. We'd kept the faith throughout the long dark winter. We'd gone through the tunnel and stepped out into the light of Tony's dazzling teeth. Labour was going to abolish the House of Lords and reform the electoral system. It was going to wipe out zero-hours contracts. It was going to tackle tax evasion and bring the City of London to heel. It was going to give Scotland home rule. Labour was going to do all the things that it tells us it's going to do this time. That's the real reason that Tony Blair is the man who cannot be mentioned, and not because he's the Middle East peace envoy who applauds wars and does deals with torturers.

This time, the promises are not made with Tony's doe-eyes and fake bonhomie: they come to us courtesy of the staring eyes of Jim Murphy and his dancing eyebrows which promise every flavour of jam to every man, woman and child. Jim Murphy, the Labour Party's peace envoy to Scotland. Jim gives us his word, the man who thinks the neoconservative Henry Jackson Society is a leading light in the struggle for social justice. Throw in a few fitba references Jim, and then we'll be convinced. Keepie-uppie, Celtic, sweating while the goalposts shift. Well colour me confident heid-the-baw Jim. Jim is what happens when the politics of Tony Blair de-evolve and return to the primordial slime.

Tony Blair is why Labour can't be trusted with the absolute power that a Westminster majority grants. He showed us that once Labour gets total power it forgets what it's supposed to stand for. Jim and his dancing eyebrows and kaleidoscope of promises are another symptom of Labour's old disease. And that's why we can't let them get total power ever again. Scotland needs to hold Labour to account, and the only way we can do that in a Westminster first-past-the-post election (sorry Greens and SSP) is by voting SNP.

Labour in Scotland are staring into the abyss eroded out by Tony's lies, by Gordie's delusions and vows, by the cheers Alistair Darling received at the Tory conference, by the frantically spinning eyebrows of Jim. In a few short weeks the voters of Scotland will push them over the edge, and once they fall there will be no way back. Their grave will be marked by the tombstone teeth of Tony.

9 April 2015

Jim will be swatted from history by the voters

Poor Jim Murphy, it's been a rough week. Even BBC Scotland couldn't avoid a mention of his troubles — just the one mention, very very briefly and sandwiched between stories about murrdurrs, cute fluffy kittens, and lots and lots of fitba so if you blinked you'd have missed it, but still.

When even BBC Scotland has to acknowledge that Jim isn't driving Labour's battlebus along a highway to an ever more perfect Union, then you know something has gone very seriously wrong. And it has. Jim's campaign is now roadkill, the battlebus is buggerbust. Not that I'm accusing the BBC Scotland news and current affairs management team of being biased, not at all. But then tabloid newspapers that print vows in faux parchment script don't think they're biased either. Me, I'm totally biased. But at least I'm honest about it.

Anyway, after being publicly slapped on the face with an austerity fish by Ed Baws then chucked under that battlebus by Chuka Umunna, and seeing Labour's popularity plummet in a Scottish opinion poll to near Cleggesque levels, James Francis Murphy, BA Politics (failed), is now envious that Ed Miliband only has to contend with a video of him picking his nose. Jim would give anything for that problem, whereas his problems have been caused by the fact that he's spent the past five months digging all his policies out of a different orifice entirely. Now things have got so bad that Jim has been forced to attack the Tories instead of the SNP.

Jim taking over as branch manager hasn't worked out according to the exultant predictions in the UK press. Jim was the big hitter who was going to show those provincial politicians how the big boys did things. He'd put the nationalist genie back in the Buckie bottle and deep-fry their Mars bars. Jim would save Scotland for the Union and lazy Caledonian stereotypes. The metrocommentariat said that the only reason the uppity separatists were guffawing so loudly was because they were terrified by Jim and his big-hitty thing. Jim would put those nationalists in their place. They knew this because a press release from Jim's publicity people had told them so, so it had to be true. Jim wouldn't lie.

But the big boy has had his backside kicked by the wee lassie with the tin hat. That wasn't supposed to happen. Shoutiness hasn't worked, patronising condescension hasn't worked, scare stories haven't worked, smears haven't worked, promises of jam haven't worked, even Scottish Labour's favourite fallback tactic of flat out lying hasn't worked. They always worked in the past because the party could rely on a tsunami of favourable press coverage from the Scottish media, and especially from BBC Scotland. But we had a referendum last year, and Scotland learned how to surf.

All that Jim has left is to try to rerun the referendum campaign and hope for some eggs so he can pose as a protector of Unionist poultry. But Jim's chickens have come home to roost, and the only thing flying thick and fast is the guano. Most of which is landing on Jim.

It was revealed this week that Jim has a police presence at Labour events to defend the defender of the Union against any ovoid assaults. There isn't any police presence at Lib Dem events; some unkind souls have suggested that this is because the Lib Dems haven't paid the polis for policing the Lib Dem conference and the polis are quite happy for Wullie Rennie and the Number 19 bus to Kelty to remain unprotected. It is in fact because attacking the Lib Dems is like attacking a dodo: it's already extinct so there's no point. Just look at Alistair Carmichael, who is pointlessness on a smeary plate.

After being telt by the Eds and chucked by Chuka, Jim felt the need to recoup a sliver of his authority. Following Labour's real leadership's announcement that the leader of the party in Scotland didn't get to determine the UK budget, Jim tweeted that he was in charge of how the money was spent in Scotland. Not the Scottish government apparently. All that devolution, and the most powerful person in the land is a Labour backbencher. Was that a part of the rapidly unravelling Vow as well? Jim didn't clarify, he'd quickly moved on to yelling at the Tories and hoping that Scottish voters have forgotten how he was cosying up to the Tories just a few short months ago, and indeed spent most of the recent rammython on the BBC Politics show high-fiving Ruth Davidson and ganging up with her against Nicla.

Earlier this week the Tory manifesto included a provision to strip Scottish MPs of the right to vote on income tax bands in the Commons. It's a betrayal of the Smith Commission yelled Jim, glad he had something to shout about as a distraction technique. Jim knows a lot about betraying the Smith Commission as he and his party spent most of the negotiations gutting any proposals for the meaningful devolution of extra powers and doing their utmost to reduce it to the absolute minimum that they could get away with. Power over the minimum wage? Oh you can't have that. Power over abortion? That's not going to happen. Control over broadcasting? Not even on the test card.

For Labour, the Smith Commission was an exercise in extracting party political advantage and not about responding to what Scotland wants, and now they're complaining that the Tories are doing exactly the same thing.

Jim has run out of tactics and the battlebus has run out of road. His midgie strategy of producing a cloud of wee nasty bites which would draw the SNP's blood has failed miserably. No one likes midgies and in any case forty-five per cent of the Scottish population are genetically immune to midgie bites. Considerably more are immune to the blandishments of Jim, but that's what happens after you've spent the past twenty years of your political career out-Blairing Tony Blair, and then you claim to be a socialist. The lesson for Labour in this campaign is

that even midgies are more popular than hypocrites.
On 7 May we'll be getting out the fly spray.

16 April 2015

Death goes on the stump with Jim

We must be living in End Times, when cats lie down with dogs, birds fall from the skies, day turns into night, the BBC is unbiased, Katie Hopkins says something compassionate and empathetic — well maybe not those last two — but Norman Tebbit really has called on people in Scotland to vote Labour. Tebbit, that Tebbit, the on-your-bike Tebbit, the only person more evilly Thatcherite than the Thatch herself, wants people in Scotland to vote Labour in order to keep out the SNP. Just sit and absorb that quietly for a few moments, if you can. Alternatively you can absorb it while screaming inchoately in rage, anger and grief, which is what I did.

Tebbit was the evil uncaring embodiment of an evil and uncaring government which already had evil and uncaring off pat entirely without his assistance. Tebbit was the bitter icing on a rancid cake of greed and rancour. He was Iain Duncan Smith without the compassion, Michael Gove without the social conscience, George Osborne without the joie de gimp. And he wants you to vote Labour.

Norm doesn't have a very high opinion of the Scottish Tories. He thinks that the Tories in Scotland should just give up and disband, a sentiment many of us share. Where we disagree is that Norm wants a new party to form in Scotland, a Unionist one like they have in Northern Ireland. Apparently Scottish politics could do with a bit more mindless sectarianism, intolerant religious fundamentalism and saying NO! to things. Norman doesn't like our resolutely peaceful and democratic approach to mass participatory politics, he wants a few more flute bands and ill-fitting uniforms. It might damage Scottish public life, but it would benefit the Tory party in Westminster and that's all Norman cares about.

Norm said: "What is needed in Scotland from the Tories' point of view is to wrap up the Conservative Party and put down a little bit of fertiliser on the ground to encourage the growth of a Scottish Unionist party." It's not really clear why Norm thinks this will help; the Tories have been throwing crap at Scotland for decades now and it's not done them any good. So having given up on the hapless Scottish Tories, Norm has turned his attentions to Jim Murphy and his not so merry band of muppets.

But there's no sign of a new Tory party coming along any time soon, certainly not in time to save Westminster from the hordes of Scottish people about to descend on it and demand an input into British politics. That the pit bull of Thatcher has advised people to vote Labour says a lot about the duplicitous and underhand nature of Tebbit's approach to politics. But then, it says a whole lot more about the Labour Party in Scotland, none of which is good.

All across Labour's traditional heartlands people have been finding some very good words to say about the Labour Party; unfortunately for the Labour Party none of them can be printed in the pages of a family newspaper. How low has Labour in Scotland sunk, how far removed has it got from its socialist roots, how distant from the dreams of Keir Hardie, for Norman Tebbit to advise people to vote for it.

Norman Tebbit wants people to vote for Jim Murphy, that's the endorsement of death. Jim would be as well to have your actual Death turning up at people's doors and canvassing for him with a scythe and a bicycle. Vote Labour, or your pension will get on a bike and die. Oh wait, they've already said that haven't they.

So that's now two of the Four Horsemen of the Jockalypse who are openly riding for Labour, as we've known for quite some time that Jim's a big fan of War.

Meanwhile Pestilence has been booked to speak for its spiritual twins, Magrit Curran and Ian Davidson. Thankfully, as is typical of Labour election events, entry is by invitation only and tickets are only available for those who are already infected, otherwise there would be a run on sales of Dettol and bleach at Parkhead Forge as concerned residents struggled to contain the outbreak. Although this is of course entirely unnecessary, as anyone with any sense knows that Labour can be contained with a sneer and a spot of contemptuous dismissal — which is precisely the medicine they've been dishing out to working-class Scottish communities for decades. Sneering and contemptuous dismissal are now rampant across Labour's traditional heartlands. They've only got themselves to blame for showing us how to do it.

That just leaves Famine, who was last seen looking

for a sandwich in a branch of Subway near Glasgow Central station.

Undaunted, or more likely utterly desperate and out of ideas, Jim Murphy, in an attempt to regain the glory days when he stood on top of an Irn Bru crate, and the world — or at least the media — was at his feet, was at it again yesterday, studiously avoiding any recommendations from Norman. Jim went to St Enoch's in Glasgow, named after an imaginary saint, to stand on his Irn Bru crate and bellow his imaginary socialism through a megaphone at an imaginary crowd. St Enoch is the patron saint of utter desperation, serial liars and moral decay so it was all deeply appropriate. Admittedly I just made that up, but then Jim has invented his entire politics so fair's fair.

There was no one to listen to him in the Glasgow sun except a tight little shell of Labour activists guarding him against any stray eggs. The cameras focused in tightly to disguise the fact that Jim was shouting at himself, his words drifting away in the air and only the doos paying attention. It's hard being the saviour of the Union when no one cares.

The shoppers scurried past, more interested in a buy-one-get-one-free offer from a cheap clothing store than in Jim's cheap impression of social democracy, manufactured in the sweatshop of a focus group. He's only been wearing it for a week or so, and already it's thin and threadbare. It doesn't sit well on him. Poking through the rips and tears, we can see the bones of Norman Tebbit, setting Labour on its bike to the grave.

23 April 2015

SNP: Mad, bad and dangerous you know

In case you've just landed from another planet and haven't been following the election campaign as covered by the newspapers dahn sarf, the SNP are bad. They're really really bad. The bad bad SNP are badly bad, and Scottish people have gone collectively insane by supporting the bad SNP and the most dangerous woman in Britain. No Barbie doll is safe you know.

But they don't care, those hysterical bad cultishly bad, stupid Scottish people with no respect for political plastic dolls, they're listening to the bad SNP. Giving them ideas and notions that they can have an opinion that isn't the same as a *Daily Mail* editorial. They ought to listen to the voice of reason instead, that would be our editorial voice, telling them that they're a bit rubbish. Scotland is not bad, just pathetic. Now let's toss them a Barnett formula deep-fried heroin Mars bar and they'll sit down and be quiet and we'll hear no more about it.

Despite a campaign of fear, smear and demonisation unprecedented since the last time there was a campaign of fear, smear and demonisation — which was only a few months ago — the media onslaught has not dented the inexorable rise of the SNP in Scottish opinion polling. If anything, it's given it a boost in that very Scottish "oh ye bluidy think so, ah'll show ye then" sort of a way.

Labour had predicted that in the last days of the general election campaign there would be a swing in the polls, and they were right. It's just not been a swing in the direction they were hoping for. And those polls they just keep on swinging. Swinging like a prize boxer punching Labour's hopes of re-election in the gob.

This week, a poll was released which showed that the SNP could even sweep the board and hoover up every single seat in Scotland. The SNP has broken the political system again with a swing that has never been seen before; they're the sultans of swing and they're doing it on purpose, swinging swingeing and singing.

Poor Labour, it don't mean a thing if you ain't got that swing. It's the worst crisis since the abdication, according to Teresa May, because the SNP getting most seats in Scotland is clearly worse than WWII and the Blitz. It's worse than the worst financial crisis since the Great Depression. It's even worse than making the discovery that you're older than Nigel Farage. But arguing that the SNP can play no role in the government of the UK is an admission that Scotland is already another country.

Already there are calls from some quarters that the first-past-the-post system has to be reformed. Labour and the Tories were quite happy to put up with its unfairness as long as they were the beneficiaries, but now that someone else is benefitting, that's unfairly unfair and can't be allowed. Does anyone want to bet that they'll only propose to change the voting system for Westminster elections in Scotland?

In Scotland Labour's vote share is now just a few points ahead of the Tories. This is not because the Tories are doing any better, it's because in terms of their appeal to the Scottish electorate, Labour are as attractive as a deep-fried scab from a mongrel with mange. The party is blessed with the Samid touch: everything they touch turns to dlog, which is an ancient Celtic word meaning "less popular than a 1970s BBC Radio DJ". Gaelic is such an expressive language, isn't it?

According to Sky News, Jim Murphy, BA Politics (failed), who is Labour's branch office manager in Scotland — at least this week — received the news that he could be about to lose his job while he danced the hokey-cokey in a retirement home for the benefit of some telly cameras. Still it was nice to see that he was getting in some practice for his future career. Nero fiddled while Rome burned, and Jim danced desperately like your dad at a wedding while Labour dissolved in the public's disgust. Putting their right leg in because they don't have a left. In, out, and shaking it all about, but mostly out. He's got no sense of rhythm but it's the closest he's got to a swing. Jim is a man with his future behind him and Labour is the party of the pensioned-off. Dad-dancing Jim is the image that's going to define this campaign for the Labour Party in Scotland.

This is happening because of the demonisation and the hatred. It's happening because the Tory press and media is telling Middle England to be afraid of

Alicsammin, who's a worse crisis than ISIS. Davie Cameron and Lynton Crosby think that it works to their advantage, Scotland is a pawn that they can sacrifice in pursuit of votes in England, so they play up the SNP scare. And all the while they hammer a wedge into the cracks in the Union.

Scotland is not the audience for this message, but we hear it loud and clear. We hear that we can be sacrificed. Davie is in for a big shock. It's not Alicsammin he ought to be afraid of, it's all those Scottish people who are going to vote for a party which will rewrite the rules of a game — one that the Tories and Labour have rigged in their own favour for generations — and use it to secure what's best for Scotland. This time, Scotland is going to demand what it's due: we've tried asking nicely, we've tried playing by Westminster's rules. Now Westminster will play by ours.

It's not over yet, polls are not votes. There's still a week to go and a week is famously a long time in politics, but it's hard to see what Labour can do at this late state to turn things around. It's clear where the momentum lies. It lies with the party with rhythm, it lies with the sultans of swing, not the embarrassing dad dancer in the retirement home.

30 April 2015

It's the end of days for those who shut us out

Last summer a nation was in movement, on the march from door to door, to public meetings, to church halls and city streets. The air was full of the prospect of change, of dreams that shimmered with the solidity of truth. After decades of torpor, Scotland had learned how to hope again and a nation rediscovered the real meaning of politics. Politics is that which is proper to the polity, the body of the citizenry. It's about us. Politics belongs to us, all of us first. Scotland had discovered that politics is personal, and if we want to change anything we need to change it ourselves. 2014 was Scotland's summer of hope.

Then in September an energised nation saw its hopes for a new direction get dashed on the rocks of Westminster, aided by the sirens of the media. The tide of change ebbed out, drained by fear and false promises, leaving behind the barren shifting sands of spin doctors and press calls. The Labour Party danced and clapped in celebration of the return of business as usual, of a politics that's professionalised and kept apart from the punters, while Davie Cameron told us that the real message was about England.

And then all the Unionist parties colluded together to hollow out the promises they had made in panic during the last days of the referendum campaign. Scotland was to be returned to its box. The bosses and the big boys would once again tell us what was good for us, and we would listen in silence like obedient children, grateful for the crumbs that brought no comfort.

Some of us we had a wee greet. Some of us had a few swallies. We had a few days of despondency. And then we picked ourselves up again, and said, this gemme's a bogie. It's time for a new game, a game where we the people write the rules. Scotland was on the march once more. A country had come out of the shortbread tin and there would be no going back. We'd outgrown it. We would take the Unionists at their word. Was Scotland not valued and loved? Was our voice not essential to make this Great Britain greatly British? We would demand change within the sclerotic Union, we'd pump the lifeblood through the varicose veins of Westminster.

Despite the best efforts of the ancien régime, the political landscape shifted quicker than Jim Murphy could announce fundilymundily new policies before an adoring press. The agenda would no longer be determined by spin doctors in back rooms. In an age when the audience is as media savvy as the manipulators, the era of the McTernans is over. We can see through the hype. Scotland mocked and laughed while Jim blustered and burned.

When Labour holds its press conferences and media events the people's party doesn't invite the people. The people can see they've been excluded and the people's party is no more. When we hear the politicians cry that the people are no longer listening, we remember that it's the politicians who should be listening to the people. And if they'd been listening in the first place they wouldn't be complaining now.

The people created the Labour Party to act as a force for justice and social change and it morphed into a Murph. So the people said to themselves, we did this before and we can do it again. So the people marched to another party. But no one expected the tide to return so soon and so high. Jim Murphy is being taught to beware the tides that march. They're going to wash his party away.

The notion that Scotland finds a voice has really terrified the British establishment. The only thing worse is the idea that Scotland could hold the balance of power, and determine who gets to form the next government of the UK. For the long dark decades of Tory rule, Scotland was told that getting a government we didn't vote for was simply the price of the Union. Now the tartan high heels are on the other foot, England might get the government that Scotland votes for. Ed, Davie, Nick and Nige scream that Scotland's choices are illegitimate and unwelcome. But to no avail: no one in Scotland is listening to the four hoarse men of the Jockalypse.

How dare a nation which wasn't that interested in the Royal baby have any influence in running the UK? The rivers will run with Irn Bru, and cucumber sandwiches will be abolished and replaced by bridies. Taxi drivers in Sussex will be forced to accept Scottish banknotes. Wee yappy Scottie dugs will run wild in the streets of Winchester. But worst of all, a party which in the cosmic scheme of things isn't especially left wing will drag Labour back from its ever rightward triangulation dance with the Tories and end the politics of austerity that benefit only a rich minority. It's unthinkable. It's appalling. The security services have set the threat to DEFCON tartan; the Mad Macs are about to take over Westminster's blunderdome and make *Daily Mail* columnists cry. And it's true, we're only doing it so we can see the greetin face on that wee nyaff on Sky News's *Press Preview*.

Scotland has been deluged by rejection and racism, by hatred and blind unreason coming from the uncomprehending commentators and politicians from south of the border who cannot fathom why this is happening. You'd have thought the answer was obvious. It's happening because those selfsame commentators and politicians spent last year intimidating and scaring Scotland into submission. Now Scotland is repaying the compliment. They're very scared indeed. When the media and politicians demonise you, it means you've got them scared. And that means that you are the powerful one in this equation. Scotland is showing its power.

Today Scotland holds the future of the UK in its hands. Not just the future of certain politicians' careers, satisfying as it will be to put an end to some of them. Your ballot paper is the key to a future you determine. Your pencil is a weapon that can strike through the hearts of those who've let Scotland down. Wield it well. Vote for hope. Vote for change. Vote for a positive future. Vote for a strong Scottish voice. Jockalypse now.

7 May 2015

Murph E. Coyote's fall heralds the end of the UK

Thursday's election was the best of times, it was the worst of times. It was a tale of two polities. It was the election that showed how broken Britain is. Scotland punished Labour and the Lib Dems for standing shoulder to shoulder with the Tories and preaching fear and smear. We taught them what pandafication means, black-eyed, reduced to a rump, the backside of politics. As a result the Unionist parties are on the verge of extinction, left with just one representative each — the Three Whines Men with their gifts of scold, rank insult and besmirch.

The evil Tories have won an absolute majority. Ed Balls even blamed the SNP for Labour's defeat in England. In Ed Balls's unelectable universe it's the fault of the Scots that the English voted Tory. But Labour is the agent of its own misfortune. If Labour can't persuade enough people in England to vote for it, that's not the fault of the SNP, that's the fault of Labour's rank inadequacies. The were equally complicit in the demonisation of the SNP, so only have themselves to blame for the traction that the Tories' racist scaremongering achieved.

Now we're told that Labour will have a period of reflection. We've heard all this before. It's time the party stopped confusing "a period of reflection" with looking in the mirror and thinking itself gorgeous. It's likely that Labour will now choose a figure from the party's right as its next leader, taking the party even further away from the Scottish side of the canyon. There's nothing to bridge the chasm.

The Tories will now embark upon the changes to constituency boundaries denied to them by the Lib Dems in the last parliament, and make it far easier for them to secure another absolute Tory victory in England in future. The Tories will introduce legislation to make Scottish MPs second-class representatives in Westminster. We're facing a referendum on EU membership, and might be taken out of the EU on the back of English votes. Scotland's membership of the United Kingdom was already highly conditional; with Thursday's vote Scotland became semi-detached.

If anyone thought that the question of Scottish independence had been settled by last year's indyref, Jim Murphy has got a Labour Party burst balloon to sell them. He's got a job lot of them right now.

Ed Miliband has resigned as leader of the Labour Party so he can spend more time with his family. I take full responsibility, he said. Nick Clegg has resigned as leader of the Lib Dems so he can spend more time with his family. I take full responsibility, he said. Nigel Farage has resigned as leader of UKIP so he can spend more time with David Dimbleby. I take full responsibility, he said. Jim Murphy has not resigned as leader of the Labour Party in Scotland, he's staying to spend more time with a BBC Scotland studio. It's all the fault of the SNP, he said.

Of all the party leaders who suffered defeat on Thursday, Jim's humiliation was the most complete. Labour won't lose a single seat to the SNP, Jim was claiming just a few short weeks ago. And he was correct. Labour didn't lose a single seat, it was left with a single seat. We waved goodbye to Wee Dougie. I broke my neighbours' windaes with the sonic boom of loud cheering when Magrit got her jotters. Anne McLaughlin became the Sherpa Tenzing of Scottish politics and climbed to the top of Ben Bain in Glasgow North East.

Jim claims that Labour still needs him at this difficult time, the party still has seats in the Scottish parliament that he hasn't lost for them yet. There's still more damage that he can do.

Yet Jim is still hanging on: he's not Labour's bad apple – it's their whole orchard that's rotten. Jim's a withered sour apple on a rotten apple tree. The cartoon coyote is refusing to acknowledge that he's standing on fresh air, that there's nothing to support him. He's refusing to acknowledge that he's already plunged into the canyon and there was nothing in John McTernan's ACME catalog to save him. He's equally bereft of credibility, a laughing stock. If Jim keeps those legs spinning he's hoping they can still carry him all the way to a *Reporting Scotland* studio. The leader without a seat of a party that scarcely exists any more. His leadership is now as fictional as his pre-election promises. Jim swore that he'd tell the voters of East Renfrewshire first whether he'd stand down as MP. Well they told him first. They told him his services were no longer required.

So now Jim's saying that the party needs him to provide stability, and Labour seems to be in no rush to depose him. Partly Labour's problem is that they had already scraped the bottom of the barrel when they elected Jim. If they ditch him now they've only got a few short thick planks left.

We owe the people of Scotland a debt, he said in his I'm clinging on for dear life speech. And this would be true: he owes the people of Scotland a debt of buggering off and crawling underneath a rock. There is no place left for discredited Jim in Scotland. He made a last-ditch desperate plea for tactical votes, but even the Tories of the Mearns didn't want him.

Even if every single Scot had voted Labour, we'd still be facing a Tory government. But Scotland didn't vote SNP out of nationalism. We voted for democracy. We voted for a change. We voted for a voice that would be heard. In Scotland Labour didn't lose for not being nationalist, it lost for not being left wing enough, while in England the party lost for not being right wing enough. During this election Labour described itself as the last truly British party, and like the British state, the party cannot survive this defeat in its current form. Labour tried to bestride the chasm on the dust of the Murph E. Coyote's frantic spinning, but the people saw through it. The coyote looked down and plunged to its doom, taking the fragile edifice of the British state with it. That's all folks. The UK ends in cartoon farce.

9 May 2015

47

Jim's big principle: Make me an MSP

The Nige Messiah sacrificed himself on the cross of a media interview on the Friday, and Lo! on the third day he did rise again. The worshippers of the swivel-eyed god really do believe he can walk on water. This is a miraculous feat Nige can achieve only because he steps on the heads of drowning migrants.

Meanwhile in Scotland, Jim Murphy hasn't resigned because he's been inundated with letters and messages of support. He just hasn't realised that they're all coming from SNP supporters.

The followers of the Murph E. Coyote godlet have decided to skip the sacrifice and just go straight to the granting of eternal life to the man who never appeared in a press photo without a halo on his head. In part this is because if they had walled him up in a tomb, no one would have helped them roll the stone away after the three days. And besides, there's no cave big enough to contain Jim's ego. But mainly it's because there's been a succession of Labour person-ages like Rutherglen MSP James Kelly — who's like Iain Gray without the charisma — appearing before the cameras to swear blind that Jim shouldn't resign because he fought a brilliant campaign. This does make you wonder what a rubbish campaign would have looked like. Possibly it would have entailed posting out election leaflets impregnated with the Ebola virus while Jim pulled down his troosers and mooned at Gordon Brewer during that shouty election debate. Which would at least have made it watchable.

Labour is divided amongst itself over the reason for its crushing defeat. One faction of the party thinks it's because the SNP is bad, another group believes it's because the SNP is really bad. And a third faction holds that the rout was due to the fact that the SNP is really really bad. The party now wants a period of quiet reflection so that they can decide that they lost the election because the SNP is badly evilly bad. They're not going to sack Jim because they need to think about where they went wrong, although any former Labour voter will tell them that one of the major ways they went wrong was to choose Jim as a branch office manager. Jim was even less popular in Scottish opinion polls than Davie Cameron — just how many more hints do Labour need?

Labour are now proposing to fight the 2016 Scottish elections on the dubious principle that Scotland's voters will think the best person to take responsibility for Scottish government is a man who won't take responsibility for his own party. But Jim's the perfect leader for Labour in Scotland, and if they replaced him with a socialist with principles it would be a complete betrayal of everything that the modern Labour Party in Scotland stands for.

Of course it's obvious what Jim is playing at. He's clinging on to the post of party leader like a particularly stubborn and suspicious stain left on bed sheets after a teenage make out session, because it means he'll get prime billing on Labour's list vote in next year's Holyrood elections. That's the only way he'll ever manage to get himself elected again. Jim is quite willing to sacrifice the Labour Party in order to save his own career, which will make him the first party leader in history with no party to lead. His career as a politician that anyone takes seriously is already over.

While Labour is desperately trying to save the right of a careerist to his career, human rights are under threat from a Tory government bent on abolishing the Human Rights Act and replacing it with a so-called "British Bill of Rights". The plan is being implemented by Tory injustice minister Michael Gove, who ran away from Aberdeen because even the Scottish Tories thought he was unelectable, and Scottish Tories have a wealth of experience in unelectability.

Gove wants to abolish the act as he is determined to defend proper British values like tearing a fox apart with dogs, scoffing at poor people on Great British poverty porn TV, covering up the activities of establishment paedophiles, allowing royal influence on lawmaking, cutting the benefits of people with terminal cancer, and bailing out bankers with your money. Labour has nothing to say, being preoccupied with trying to decide whether it can win the next election by being more right wing or by becoming righter wing or whether what they really need is a telegenic right-wing leader with a nice suit like Chuka Umunna.

While Labour agonises over its sartorial options,

it's the SNP which is stepping up and defending the Human Rights Act. Labour's mess is such that the SNP are the only party which is organised and coordinated enough to act as an Opposition. Not that the Tories are exactly on the ball: Paddington Mundell is the last blue panda standing, he pitched up on the steps of Westminster in a duffel coat bearing a label saying "Would someone please look after this Tory." So they gave him the job of Secretary of State for Scotland.

The Tories propose to abolish the Human Rights Act but either have forgotten or don't care that it's embedded into the devolution settlements in Scotland, Wales and Northern Ireland. In order to abolish the act, David Mundell is going to have to get the Scottish parliament to vote for its abolition in a fit of mundellirium, which is high up in the list of things which are highly improbable in this universe — like Jim Murphy standing down gracefully, or Kezia Dugdale managing to get through an interview without mentioning how bad the SNP are.

The SNP are in talks with rebel Tories to take a stand and defend the Human Rights Act, but the main battle will be between the UK goverment and the Scottish government. Scotland's rights are human rights too, and we've got a parliament sworn to defend them. The only way Westminster will be able to abolish the act throughout the UK will be by treating the Scottish parliament like Jim Murphy treats the voters of East Renfrewshire. The voters have spoken, but Jim's not listening. But if Westminster ignores the Scottish parliament in the same way, we're heading straight for a full-blown constitutional crisis which will be far more serious than any manufactured little spat on Labour's campaign trail in the streets of Glasgow.

14 May 2015

Trident is Viagra for an ageing empire

Trident whistle-blower William McNeilly is now in military custody. For many of us, he is a hero, not a criminal. He should get a medal, but he'll probably get a jail sentence for letting the public know what most of us had suspected for quite a while — that Trident is a disaster waiting to happen. An online petition to pardon William McNeilly has already received thousands of signatures. We can only hope that the government will pay attention.

Of course, nuclear warheads are designed to cause disaster, but the UK's nuclear deterrent is accidentally unsafe as well as deliberately unsafe. It's so unsafe that it might not blow up half the planet when it's supposed to, which is allegedly a bad thing, or it might blow up half of Scotland when it's not supposed to, which is definitely a bad thing.

Every day the MoD plays Rosneath roulette with Scotland's future and the future of the globe. And this is all supposed to make us feel safe. Do you feel safe? I don't. And neither did William McNeilly, who actually served on the Trident submarines, which is why he blew the whistle on the fatal farce that is the UK's nuclear deterrent.

What makes it even more galling is that there is no prize in this game of plutonium poker, it's not just

Scotland that has nothing to gain. Not using Trident means we waste billions of pounds, using Trident means we waste a world. But Scotland has everything to lose. An accident could easily pollute the Clyde forever and turn the West of Scotland into a radioactive wasteland that's uninhabitable for generations — a Faslane Fukushima with glow-in-the-dark fish suppers. The fish would be deep-fried even as they came out the water.

Not even Jackie Baillie could survive, and there are few who are thicker-skinned than Faslane's own nuclear cheerleading MSP, who claims just about every job in Dunbartonshire depends on Trident and the entire county would turn into a wasteland without it. You'd have thought that a brass neck would provide a modicum of protection against radiation poisoning, but apparently not. The only consolation is that the nuclear winter wouldn't be too bad, as it would just be normal weather for summer in Scotland.

You don't really need a whistle-blower or a Russian spy to have worked out that Trident is a clapped-out disaster zone. Every other institution of the British state is unfit for purpose, strapped for cash, short of trained staff, demoralised, managed by sociopaths, and held together with bits of Blu-Tack, wishful thinking and the rapidly diminishing supply of the magic fairy dust of public confidence which, like land and decent Scottish news programming, is not being made any more.

The MoD in particular is notorious for its cost overruns and its inability to manage projects. There is a long and depressing litany of defence projects which cost many times the original estimates and still have proven unfit for purpose. The MoD is incapable of making a toy battleship from an Airfix kit without costs overrunning by billions of pounds, and it would still sink in the bath, defeated by the forces of a rubber duck and a sponge. If the MoD was responsible for making your weans' toys, they might just be ready by the time you become a great-grand-parent. So no one ought to be surprised by William McNeilly's revelation that gluing together a Trident missile launch system was beyond them. The prob-lems of a new Astute class of submarine were well documented even before one of them came to grief on the rocks in the Kyle of Lochalsh.

Yet during the independence referendum we were assured by the defence minister that the UK's nuclear weapons were all that stood between Scotland and a possible threat from outer space. Seemingly an alien civilisation so far in advance of ours that it possesses the technology to allow it to traverse the immense distances between the stars is going to be deterred by nuclear submarines which are unable to complete a successful orbit of the Isle of Skye. CalMac ferries are more intimidating, especially when the bar runs out of drink.

These are the same people who have turned a Dalgety beach into a nuclear no-go area, and who refuse to pay for the clean-up costs or to acknowl-edge that they've done anything wrong. In this case the source of the pollution was radioactive paint, so it's easy to imagine just how reluctant they're going to be to admit to a far greater and more dangerous mess. This week the MoD issued a statement saying that "The Royal Navy disagrees with McNeilly's subjective and unsubstantiated personal views." A view is of course subjective by definition, unless you are an MoD spokespook in which case your view is vetted by the security services. McNeilly didn't release any photos or other information which could be used to further compromise the already compromised safety of the Faslane base, so of course it's unsubstantiated. The MoD wants to hide McNeilly away in a cell, and lock away concerns about Trident along with him.

But the truth is out. The Trident missile system doesn't do what it says on its £300 billion tin. It's a relic from a Cold War past but nowadays the threats we face are very different in nature. Trident is unusable, even if it could ever have been used in the first place. It exists solely as a form of Viagra for an ageing superpower which ceased to be a superpower many decades ago. It's a sexual fantasy of potency for British governments, an empire substitute for those addicted to punching above their weight. Who exactly are they supposed to be punching? They never say.

But according to William McNeilly, Trident is so unreliable that most of the time it can't be launched, so even with the danger and expense of the UK's phallic nuclear post-empire sex aid, they still can't get it up.

21 May 2015

You can tell they're lying, you see their lips move

Wednesday saw the state opening of the new parliament, which is the only time that you can get to mention Black Rods outside of gay pornography. But the nation's attention was centred upon Aliestair Carmichael, the dishonourable member for Oh-Are-You-Still-Here-Then. Aliestair is still refusing to resign — after all he only abused his position of trust as a government minister for personal and party advantage, caused a diplomatic incident, smeared the Scottish first minister in an attempt to influence the election, allowed an expensive and lengthy investigation to take place using public funds, and then lied about it.

That's nothing in comparison to what Mhairi Black has done. That Mhairi Black, she had a packet of crisps before entering parliament, and they were the expensive kind, not the cheapo ones you get in a multipack from Aldi. And I know for a fact that Natalie McGarry clapped a dog. MPs aren't allowed to clap. There's SNP hypocrisy for you.

But Aliestair must be allowed to remain in post as otherwise Scotland will become a one party state, and this would be a very bad thing. It doesn't appear to have occurred to the metrocommentariat who complain about Scotland becoming a one party state that Scots are voting SNP precisely because we were fed up with Scotland being a one party Labour state. But that one party state wasn't a bad thing, because it didn't involve putting beach towels on Dennis Skinner's seat. Actually the SNP have no need to put a beach towel on the bench, as Dennis's seat is haunted by all the dead people he allowed to vote in the 1979 referendum when he supported the infamous forty per cent rule.

The state opening of parliament is a glittering occasion when democracy is celebrated by the ceremonial leaking of the government memo. The other ritual, the ritual heckle from the honourable Beast of Bolsover, didn't happen this year because the beast had to get up early and put his beach towel on the front bench before the SNP tourists got there so he was too knackered to think of any witticisms. But not to worry, this still allowed the other-other ritual: the ritual smearing of the SNP in the British press.

The centrepiece of the day was the Queen's Speech, when an elderly multimillionaire dripping with eye-wateringly expensive jewellery, which even a rap singer would think a bit over the top in the bling department, waltzed into a palace surrounded by flunkies in costume, and then sat on a throne to give a speech about austerity.

As is the custom, she didn't write the speech herself: it was handily written for her by her government — those men and women that Malcolm Bruce assures us are compulsive liars. The richest woman in the country tells the rest of us that there's no money to pay for poor people's needs, but no need to tax rich people. We're getting those lies in early this year. This prospectus has been agreed by about a quarter of the electorate of the UK, and about a tenth of that in Scotland. And then they wonder why the public are losing faith in the Westminster system.

The headline was the Tory plan for an EU referendum and what the Tories are pleased to call a programme for social justice. No really. Social justice is what the Tories call demonising poor people and blaming them for the mess that the unregulated financial industry got us all into.

An essential part of Tory social justice is welfare reform. That's reforming the benefits system in the same sense that when you undermine a house's foundations, rip off half the roof tiles, tear out the wiring and pipes and flog them off to a scrapyard, and demolish the bedroom then you are engaged in renovations. Tories don't like to talk about benefits — they prefer to use the American term and speak of welfare, a word which is associated with mental images of charitable handouts without any rights or entitlement. The only entitlements in the UK are those enjoyed by politicians and the rich. It's language which the Labour Party has also adopted. They're trying to reform public attitudes to the poor, and sadly succeeding.

The speech was more notable for what it didn't contain than for what it did. Somewhat like Davie Cameron's moral principles really. The foxes got away for another day, and the bonkers plan to abolish the Human Rights Act was quietly brushed under the Queen's million quid sparkly hat.

The speech mentioned devolution for Scotland eventually, but only the absolute minimum of devolution. Even then we first had to listen to promises about devolution for England and HS2, so it's nice to know where we stand in Davie Cameron's list of priorities. We mustn't complain, as he did announce on the day after the Scottish referendum that the real lesson the UK government had learned was that it had to think about English votes.

However on the positive side the speech did also include a promise that the UK government would work with the Scottish government on a basis of common respect. There's another of those lies that Malkie told us about — that didn't take long then, did it? Probably they mean common respect in the Aliestair Carmichael sense.

During last year's independence referendum we were told that if we voted Yes then the super-duper high-speed railway line wouldn't come to Scotland. This week we were told that it won't be coming to Scotland because there is no business case for it. Presumably this must also mean that there is no business case for Scotland remaining in the Union. When the Channel Tunnel was built we were promised that it would eventually be possible to travel from Scotland and the North of England direct to Europe by high-speed train, but that turned out to be another of those lies that Malkie told us about.

Transport is supposed to be the means by which different parts of the UK are joined to one another, but there is no joined-up thinking in UK transport planning. HS2 won't connect with HS1, which goes from St Pancras to the Channel Tunnel. There's not much evidence of any joined-up thinking in the Tories' Queen's Speech either, which is why Scotland is growing ever more disconnected from the Union.

28 May 2015

A bill that's as fishy as a YO! Sushi menu

The UK government has published the bill to give Scotland more powers, or so they're saying. Unfortunately, and entirely accidentally, the bill itself is harder to read and comprehend than flat-pack furniture instructions written in Japanese by a dyslexic computer programmer whose sole knowledge of the Japanese language derives from a YO! Sushi menu. So we just have to take Davie Cameron's word for it that the bill fully implements the recommendations of the Smith Commission and makes Scotland the devolviest devolved country in the history of devolviness.

Based on Davie's previous interventions in the devolution debate, however, it's quite likely that his understanding of Scotland also derives from a YO! Sushi menu. This accounts for why he thinks he can get away with fobbing us off with a slap across the face with a small bit of raw fish in lieu of a lasting devolution settlement. We can have a little morsel, but it's not going to quench the appetite. Within the Union Scotland is doomed to remain the poor wee orphan saying "Please sir can I have some more?"

It's not beyond the wit of even the Westminster parliament to produce a draft devolution bill that can be read and understood by an interested punter.

Instead the bill has been drafted in such a way as to make it impossible to understand unless it is carefully cross-referenced with previous devolution bills, papers lodged in the basement of the Palace of Westminster, and the horoscope page of a tabloid newspaper. What this tells us is that Scotland will only get proper devolution from Westminster when Mundell is in conjunction with Uranus.

None of this should come as a surprise of course. These are Tories we're talking about here. That's the party whose Scottish leader posed on a tank in the hope of scaring opponents into forgetting that her Scottish policies consisted of resurrecting the ghost of Thatcher, who was also fond of posing on tanks. The opacity of the bill is not unrelated to the fact that with this Tory government we've got a man in charge of social security who wants to strip all sociability and security from the social security system, another who is bent on stripping the country of human rights protections from injustice in charge of justice, a woman who voted twice against gay marriage in charge of equality, and a fluffy party balloon who is a dedicated opponent to devolution in charge of a new devolution settlement.

The UK government doesn't want to publish the bill in clear and simple language because then the likes of you and me would understand it, and we won't be happy. If they honestly believed that Scotland would welcome the bill with an outpouring of grateful relief and that we'd hold all those street parties we couldn't be bothered to hold during the Royal Wedding then they'd publish the bill in Ladybird

Book format and get Dale Winton to announce that every lottery ticket sold in Scotland would come with a free Barnett subsidy.

Instead we've got a supposedly democratic government publishing a document that the demos can't understand. There's always a reason for that. The centrepiece of the bill is an attempt to neuter the Scottish government. It's a con, a sleight of hand performed by the cack-handed. No one has ever looked upon David Mundell and accused him of being deft, except perhaps in the leafier suburbs of Edinburgh where they famously believe that sex is something that coal is delivered in.

With these new super-duper devo-maxiest powers that we were promised with the last desperate Unionist draws on the fag end on the referendum campaign, Scotland will be granted highly limited powers over benefits. In theory the Scottish parliament could rule that it was going to protect vulnerable people whose incomes have been slashed by the sanctions vampires of Iain Duncan Smith, but Scotland will only be able to implement any of these protections by raising income tax. No other substantial taxation powers are being given to Scotland, so we won't have the full range of tax raising powers available to Westminster. No Scottish control over National Insurance, VAT, corporation tax or the rest. Just the tax that directly affects ordinary working people most immediately in their pay packets.

The playing field is perfectly level, it's just vertical, and it's Scotland's poor and disabled who will fall off the cliff while Labour and the Tories tell Holyrood that it has the power to stop it happening. They'll blame the Scottish government for not catching the wheelchair when it's them who took off the brake and gave it a shove over the edge.

Scotland is going to be given ten metres of rope in order to rescue people who have been thrown over a two-hundred-metre cliff. And we still won't be able to do anything to stop those who're throwing the people off the cliff in the first place. Meanwhile the Unionists will blame the Scottish government for the pile of splattered and bloody bodies piling up in the deep chasms of poverty and exclusion and hope to hoover up the votes from the devotees of poverty porn on the undevolved telly.

It's funny how broadcasting never managed to make it into the Unionist definition of most devolved administration ever. The Basque Country, Catalonia, Greenland — even tiny Gagauzia with its population of just 155,000 in the poorest corner of Moldova, the poorest country in Europe — have control over broadcasting. But not the supposedly most devolved country in the history of devolviness. And then you remember BBC Scotland's coverage of the referendum and you realise why.

The price for these non-protections dressed up as substantial new powers and no Scottish media platform to debate or discuss them will be stripping Scottish MPs of their power to vote on key parts of the UK budget under the guise of English votes for English laws. Because if you sincerely believe that Scotland depends upon subsidies from England, then you're also going to believe that Scotland has no right to have a say on the overall UK budget. Scotland is just another wheelchair for the Tories to push over the edge.

This is exactly the kind of underhand sleekitness that destroyed Scotland's faith in the Unionist parties and the Westminster parliament to begin with. They just keep doing it. They can't help themselves. They don't know any other way of being. Their image is as toxic as FIFA's, but they're not being investigated and no one is going to resign. Alistair Carmichael is still with us — just pointing that out. The day is getting ever sooner when Scotland calls that the gemme is a bogie and goes to play in an independent league.

4 June 2015

What's the point of the Labour Party?

Labour was once a machine, now it's a broken bit of stick and some frayed string wrapped around a yo-yo that's lost its yo. Does anyone know what Labour is for? Other than acting as a work placement scheme for the terminally careerist of course — although it's not even functioning as that any more as Labour's careerists' careers have yoed their last.

Rumour has it that Jim Murphy is currently plotting how to shoo out some Labour list MSPs so he can attempt a reboot of some of the usual suspects who were booted during the Westminster election. We can at least be certain that it's the usual cobblers.

Following the resignation of Ed Miliband, and the eventual acknowledgement of Jim Murphy that he could resign now that Alistair Carmichael has trumped him in the out of touch and mendaciousness stakes, the party is too consumed with its own internal politicking to concern itself with the ordinary punters. Which, to be honest, isn't really any different from what it's been doing for the past few decades. So at the moment, policy-wise Labour is a blank canvass, a look which goes well with their blank minds as they try to work out just what went so catastrophically wrong.

Although Labour is flailing around wildly as it tries

to decide whether the key to becoming electable in England is to tack a little to the right, a lot to the right, or to go full out raving tabloid, they have managed to reveal their new Scottish policy, designed to make them re-electable north of the border.

The policy was revealed by Ian Murray, the Shadow Scotland Secretary and the MP for Red Morningside, and consists of screaming SNPBAD!! with two exclamation marks instead of the previous one. It's that extra exclamation mark which is going to make all the difference to Labour's electoral prospects. And when the party is feeling the pressure, they have a super-secret policy weapon — SNPBAD!!! with three exclamation marks. Scottish leadership candidate Kezia Dugdale is confident that it's going to make that crucial difference and doesn't make the party look like a crazy person pushing a shopping trolley and yelling abuse at imaginary demons. Oh no, not at all.

However just in case the new policy is not a raging success, Kezia has a backup plan and has legally changed her name to Kezia!! in the hope that she'll be mistaken for a musical. Although there already is a musical about the Labour Party in Scotland, it's called *Les Misérables* — which is a pity as Jim Murphy had been rehearsing for the role of the Lying King. If he had been allowed to wear the lion mask and sing "Howkin Ma Tattie" during the election debate, he may actually have persuaded some voters that his working-class credentials were genuine, and electoral history could have been completely different.

But now it's all on the shoulders of Dippity

Dugdale as front runner in the leadership contest to save the party. The entirely unmemorable Ken MacWossisname has no chance — since no one can remember his name, his chances of coming up with a catchy tune or catchy policies are pretty much zero.

If all else fails, Kezia!! can host a reality contest on BBC Scotland seeking someone to play the lead role in the musical tragedy of Labour's life, sending the survivors of the first round off to a boot camp run by Jackie Baillie. Some of the more despondent amongst the shattered remnants of the party believe it is entirely possible that this is the change to the leadership selection process that Jim Murphy is going to suggest in his review. Although it's going to take quite a spectacular sob story involving a dying granny with dysentery who fell off a cliff in a wheelchair and crushed a limping puppy before anyone can look more greetin faced than Kezia!! does at *First Minister's Questions* every week.

The new exclamation mark was unveiled the day before a devastating opinion poll showing that Labour is set to lose all its constituency seats and be left with a rump of just twenty-five list seats at the next Scottish elections. Fully sixty per cent of Scottish voters have not been persuaded by the old SNPBAD! message, so that extra exclamation mark in the entirely new and totally different SNPBAD!! policy is going to have to do a lot of heavy lifting.

The other policy that Labour hopes will save it has been described as an extension of devolution. At least it's been described as such by the same kind of demented zoomers who informed us that the

infamous Vow was super-duper devo-maxiest federalism. Which is pretty much most of the mainstream
media in Scotland.

Don't get the wrong idea though, heaven forfend
that Labour might consider taking powers away from
Westminster and transferring them to Holyrood,
which is the definition of extending devolution as
understood by people who speak human. Oh no,
this special Labour extension of devolution actually
means stripping the Scottish parliament of powers,
and in this case passing those powers on to local
authorities — which entirely coincidentally is the
only sector of government where Labour still retains
a bit of a power base. So it's not about what Scotland
wants or needs, boys and girls, it's about what's good
for the Labour Party.

You'd think that by now Labour would have worked
out that adopting policies that are good for the Labour
Party but not good for the voters is counterproduc-
tive and ends up not being good for the Labour Party
after all. But they just can't help themselves, and are
locked into a cycle of self-destructive behaviour.

Meanwhile this week in the Commons, Labour
either abstains or votes with the Tories to deny votes
to sixteen- and seventeen-year-olds in the EU referendum. Labour hasn't worked out that we don't need
another off-key right-wing neoconservative British
nationalist party; we've already got the Tories for
that — and they don't exactly sing to the Scottish
electorate. It's no wonder that no one knows what
the Labour Party is for: Labour doesn't know itself.

11 June 2015

1 + 1 + 1 = 57

Unionist arithmetic says that $1 + 1 + 1 = 57$. What the three Unionist MPs elected by Scotland vote for outweighs what the fifty-six SNP MPs vote for. This is what last year's Better Together campaign meant by punching above our weight. That's the only possible explanation for what happened in Westminster on Monday evening. We were warned before the election that the SNP was going to hold the UK to ransom; afterwards we discovered that it is the UK parties which are holding Scotland to ransom.

The Unionist parties voted down an SNP amendment seeking to introduce the wide-ranging and substantial devolution which the Unionist parties had promised in the last frantic days of the referendum campaign, and the Conservatives reneged on their promise in the notorious vow to make the Scottish parliament permanent. The Vow lied, and the Smith Commission died.

The Unionists promised us these things in order to secure a No vote in the referendum, and having secured their No they wheeched the offer away. The Tories voted down the very first line in Gordie Broon's Vow and the foundation of the Smith Commission agreement: to make the Scottish parliament permanent. An SNP amendment sought to introduce into law the principle that Westminster could only abolish Holyrood after Scotland's voters had given consent in a referendum, but Westminster said no. It determined that it would reserve to itself the right to abolish the Scottish parliament, irrespective of what the Scottish people want. It's the principle of the thing, said a Westminster which thinks it's too dangerous to allow the people the principle of democracy. If they've shown themselves to be untrustworthy on the very first line of their Vow, how can they be trusted to deliver the rest of it?

You'd think that treating the very first line in the Vow as a disposable nappy would count as news in a media that prides itself on holding politicians to account — the same media that hounds the SNP over every perceived misrepresentation of actualities that often only exist in the imagination of a journalist with an agenda and an axe to grind. But this week we were presented with the undeniable trashing of a core promise in a Unionist manifesto that was headline news for a week on BBC Scotland, yet Scotland's public broadcaster doesn't see fit to mention it.

And with that the heart was ripped out of the Union. Now we're just waiting for the death message to make its way along the decaying spinal cord to the spongiform half-conscious brain. Westminster can't say it wasn't warned, Bad Vow Disease is invariably fatal. This counts as a material change of circumstances. We're no longer in the Union that we were told we were. The Union of the Vow is a myth.

That wasn't the only Smith myth on offer this week. The new Scotland Office Secretary has been taking honesty lessons from his predecessor. "It is a myth that Gordie Broon called for either federalism or home rule," said Paddington Mundell during the debate, trying to create a new myth of his own. Mundell may well try to deny what Gordie Broon said, but it was widely quoted and repeated on the same undevolved national broadcaster which is now overlooking Mundell's misrepresentation of the truth, just like it's ignoring what's happening with the Scotland Bill.

This is the second time within a few days that the Fluffy One has either been confused or attempted to dissemble, although to be fair those two possibilities are not mutually exclusive. Last week he claimed that there was no Scotland Office veto in legislation that says that the Scottish government must consult with and get the permission of the Scotland Office before it can use certain powers. Which is another way of saying veto. But Fluffy thinks that it can't be a veto unless the word "veto" is actually used and someone from the Scottish Office rushes into the chamber of the Scottish parliament screaming Nooooooooo! It's Mundelly fundilimentalist, which is a peculiar form of literalism that is more usually associated with religious fundamentalists who say that the world is only six thousand years old and dinosaurs walked amongst human beings. Although when you look at the Conservative and Labour benches in the Commons you can see that they still do.

Watching the progress of the Scotland Bill was a dismal and depressive sight. Again and again, small, tiny steps towards a surer-footed Union were laughed into irrelevance by the braying voices of a triumphalist Tory party that doesn't need to care. Scotland, you'll get what you are given and you'll be grateful for it. The Smith Commission is what the Tories say it is, and the general election in Scotland may just as well have never happened. The Scottish people spoke, but they spoke to a deaf ear, a deadened mind and a clenched fist that won't let go of any power or control.

And what was Labour doing while all this was going on? It was pooling, sharing and abstaining. After screaming at us for months about the evils of FFA they did sweet FA. Abstention is the new opposition — like a sulking teenager which has taken to its bedroom screaming that it's all unfair, Labour can't be bothered voting against the Tories.

On Tuesday, Labour's failure to do the job that they were elected to do handed a victory to the Tory government. Davie Cameron wants to suspend the purdah period during the last days of the EU referendum. This rule is supposed to prevent the government introducing material changes to any offers in the final days of the vote — when postal voting has already begun and many people will have already cast their ballot. Mind you, the existence of the purdah period didn't stop them from making the Vow during the last days of the Scottish referendum. The SNP voted to block the government's move, as did a group of Tory backbench rebels. If Labour had bothered to turn up, the government would have lost this crucial vote, but Labour was too busy sitting in the Commons' bars and tea rooms harrumphing to itself.

We have a government that only a tiny minority of Scots voted for, and an official Opposition that scarcely any more voted for — and it can't be bothered turning up to oppose. Our politics have gone beyond satire and are now a tragedy, one which will end with the death of the UK.

25 June 2015

Westminster says naw

Before the referendum Davie Cameron said, "If Scotland says it does want to stay inside the United Kingdom then all the options of devolution are there and are possible." Ed Miliband, when he was still leader of the Labour Party, promised that a No vote would deliver "faster, better and safer change". We could have devo max and home rule, and the closest thing to full-frontal federalism possible (©Gordie Broon); full fiscal autonomy was clearly on the table. But it was all a part of the traditional game of bait-and-switch that the Westminster parliament plays with Scottish aspirations. The empty shell was revealed this week: all that's on offer is a dismissive sneer and a guffaw of contempt. This is democracy in Scotland.

On Monday night an empty House of Commons debated more devolution for Scotland — the only benches that were full were the SNP ones, the sidelined majority of Scotland's representatives. Scotland's official voice is the Tory one, because that's what England voted for. Scotland's official Opposition is the Labour one, because that's what England voted for. So the Tory one and the Labour one played their irrelevant games of back and forth, trying to score points in their favourite sport of SNP condemned, because that's what England voted for. Pointing all this out is of course racist. The handful of English MPs in attendance made interjections which might have come from Mars for all the awareness they displayed of Scotland's issues. According to one Labour MP, Scotland shouldn't have control of air passenger duty because of HS2, apparently unaware that it comes nowhere near Scotland and probably never will.

Then after a couple of hours of mind-numbing intelligence insulting, the matter of full fiscal autonomy actually came to a vote, and 504 MPs who don't represent Scotland crawled out of the bars and ganged up on the ninety-five per cent of Scottish MPs who had just voted in favour. The bar attendees who hadn't attended the debate voted against the greater devolution that their parties had promised us in the run-up to the referendum. All the options of devolution are not there after all, and they never were. They're as mythical as Labour's parliamentary road to socialism, the one which took us to the dead-eyed end of Blair and Brown.

And then after siding with the Tories to vote down FFA, the Labour One tweeted that the SNP had voted with the Tories against a Labour proposal for an enquiry to kick a proposal that Labour don't support into the long grass. Because that's really going to get Scotland's voters back on your side, Ian Murray.

And then the MPs who don't represent Scotland cheered about denying Scotland what Scotland's MPs voted for, what Scotland's people voted for. They waved their order papers and cheered the defeat of the democratic will of an entire nation in what it pleases them to call the Mother of Parliaments. This was not a point of principle, this was not a debate hard won on fact or substance. They were cheering the fact that England is bigger than Scotland and the smaller partner's voice is drowned out by the inanities of backbench Labour and Tory MPs who know nothing and care less about the aspirations of a partner nation in the UK. The same people who tell us that it's wrong for Scotland to have a voice on English-only matters refuse to allow Scotland to have its voice on Scottish-only matters. And there was us thinking that a sense of irony was a British virtue.

The message from Westminster was clear: Scotland — you'll get what you're given and you'll damn well be grateful. And though they didn't know it, they were really cheering the death of the Union, cheering like colonialists who'd just put down a minor rebellion amongst the uppity natives who need to be told what's good for them. It's English votes for Scottish laws in this most perfect of Unions. Better Together being told what's for the best, because we can't be trusted to decide for ourselves.

The order papers waved away the last chance of Scotland rebuilding its shattered trust and its hopes that the will of its people would be respected and heard. The cheers drowned out the last chance that Scotland's voice might ever be heard. As a voter in Scotland, you regard the scene and think — what is there here for me? And the answer is nothing at all. Nothing but rejection and condescension and the stale whiff of failure. Even if the country voted as one, even if there were not even the paltry three degrees of failure of the SLab, the Tory and the Lib Dem returned from Scotland, we'd still be outvoted, still be overruled. Our democracy has become even less successful than our national football team. We have been beaten by the Faroe Islands in the devolution game. We can't even score on penalties because the only penalties are the ones we are forced to pay.

And now Scotland is paying the penalty for the majority believing in the promises of Westminster during the referendum campaign. I don't think this is what No voters were really voting for when they were told that they were voting for change. More of the same isn't change. Being told to get back in your box isn't faster, safer or better change. Watching MPs from other parts of the UK vote down the devolution settlement voted for by the people of Scotland isn't change. It's a travesty of democracy.

So now we know that Davie really meant all devolution options were "possible" in the same sense that it's theoretically possible that the atoms constituting Davie's body could simultaneously rearrange themselves into an overstuffed sofa. Although when you look at him you could be forgiven for thinking that they already had. The probability against this happening is several orders of magnitude greater than the number of atoms in the universe. By an unpleasant coincidence this is also the approximate probability that Scotland will ever get a decent devolution settlement, or indeed anything approaching democracy, out of the overstuffed sofas of the Westminster parliament.

2 July 2015

Helping the poor stand on their own feet by chopping their legs off

It's the first full-on Tory budget for almost twenty years. The tattered remnants of the Labour Party in Scotland will of course complain along with the rest of us about its unfairness, meanness and malignity. Oh if only there had been a way to avoid it entirely and protect Scotland's poor and marginalised, the low-paid and the disabled, from the onslaught of the Conservatives' ideologically driven misery. Oh wait. Yeah, there was. And it was thrown away in a worthless vow and English Votes for Everyone's Laws. Still glad you voted No then?

Those of us on the left often decry Conservative budgets as being unprincipled. Labour share this propensity too. Traditionally they're the ones who've shouted it the loudest, and they're experts on being unprincipled so we should listen to them on that one. However in this instance the accusation is unfair and untrue, because Conservative budgets are deeply principled, and Osborne's budget has faithfully adhered to a deeply traditional Tory sense of principle. In fact Labour, in its attempts to make itself electable south of the Border, looks as though it's about to adopt this principle. It's just a pity then that the principle is that the rich must be rewarded but the poor must be punished.

Being principled is not the same as being moral. Genghis Khan was a highly principled man, his favourite principle being that you gave him all your horses, your cities, your gold, and your family as slaves or he'd impale you on a stake. And if you replace the stake with a benefits sanction, then you've pretty much got Iain Duncan Smith. The only real difference is that IDS doesn't have the hair to grow a top-knot. The Tories are determined to teach the poor to stand on their own two feet, by hacking their limbs off. And in that respect they are very much like Genghis Khan.

Osborne has cut subsidies for renewable energy, but has boosted the amount to be spent on roads. Private transport gets subsidised, public transport doesn't. So no help for Scotland's struggling renewable energy sector then. After all, they want to keep taunting us about the low oil price; they certainly don't want us developing other sources of energy production.

But the main feature of this budget is the billions of cuts to benefits, the burden of which will fall on the poorest, the disabled, the people without the resources to cope, while at the same time inheritance tax has been abolished on houses worth a million and tax breaks given to those who are already comfortably off. Because it's terribly unfair that deceased rich people have to give a portion of their wealth back to the society that made them rich, and so deprive little Annabella Doublebarrelled-Surname of her Genghis Khan pony. It's appalling that people on high wages should have to pay higher rates of taxation. So if mummy and daddy are planning to leave you over a million quid when they pop their well-shod clogs, you can give a little cheer. If you're earning £40,000 a year you can now have an extra skiing holiday every year while unpaid carers try to live on £60 a week.

It's only fair: unpaid carers don't need extra skiing holidays because they can't get out the house as there's no money in social care budgets for respite care. But we mustn't complain. The cuts to the benefits budget were slightly less than the direst fears expressed beforehand, so thankfully the Tories aren't going to hack the limbs off the poor and the disabled after all. Just their legs. And their genitalia, because they certainly don't want them breeding either. There will be no tax credits for third children after 2016. Osborne's done what even Thatcher didn't dare to do — cut the link between benefits and the number of people in a household. The only boost we're going to see as a result of these changes is in the number of people who go to food banks.

The Tories hold that work is the only route out of poverty. Osborne announced a new national living wage of £7.20 per hour rising to £9 by 2020, although Osborne being Osborne there's bound to be a catch. The catch is that the minimum wage has been rebranded as the living wage, so now poverty campaigners can't use the term living wage to highlight the gap between the minimum wage and a wage you can actually live on, and the new national living wage falls a long way short of that. The living wage is currently £7.85. Every previous budget has unravelled in the following days; it's likely that this one will be no different. A fist-pumping Iain Duncan Smith looked like he was experiencing the Rapture as the news was announced. Beware of an Osborne booring git. There isn't time to do the sums yet, but I'd wager that the gains made in lower-paid income by the increased minimum wage are offset by the cuts to tax credits, and the entire announcement is a smoke and mirrors charade designed to trip up the Labour Party.

Some of the direst poverty is experienced by people who are in work. Bent on creating a low wage economy with part-time jobs and no job security, Osborne has come up with a budget that does nothing to change the bleak prospects faced by our young people. Oh if only there was a way we could escape that — right? Still, I'm sure you get the picture by now. Yes voters are feeling a mixture of despair and smug "I told you so" at this juncture. It's not much comfort, but it's all anyone's got. We've got another five years of this.

But it's not all bad. Shops can stay open for longer in England, so people there can spend longer going shopping for all the things that they can't afford. The Keep Sunday Special people are up in arms about this, as it clearly says in the Bible that thou shalt not open retail premises on the Sabbath if it hath more than 250 square metres.

This is our future, Scotland's future, a future of powerlessness in the face of Tory economic policies which penalise the poor, and it stretches before us into an infinity of gloom and despondency — unless we do something about it. That's the lesson we learn from this budget. And that something sure as hell isn't voting for a Labour Party that's in thrall to the same dismal prospect. They want us to live in the USA, but without the large portions in restaurants, the nice weather or the written constitution. Just the low wages, the insecurity, and the rampant and growing militarisation. Benefits spending bad, spending on weapons good. Welcome to Tory Britain.

9 July 2015

Protecting foxes and annoying Tories, it's all good

Many years ago I went on anti-hunt protests. I remember being smugly informed by a posh bloke that I shouldn't knock hunting until I tried it. So I set the dug on him. Or maybe I just imagined that. Being attacked by dogs isn't fun, no matter how many tally-hos and red costumes are involved. In any case, the Tories have no need of fox hunting. They've already made a sport out of hounding the poor and the homeless, and sadly that's not something that Scottish MPs are able to do anything much about. But that doesn't mean they're powerless.

This week the SNP set off on an EVEL fox hunt and succeeded in getting the Tories to think again, while greatly irritating them in the process. That's a good day at the office. Some in the independence movement have criticised them for what they regard as hypocrisy, because before the election the SNP said they wouldn't vote on English-only issues, and cited fox hunting as an example. It has been argued that this damages Scotland's right to further devolution, and even that it risks the devolution settlement that we've already got. And all, they say, over the emotive issue of a cute fluffy woodland creature.

It certainly can't be denied that allowing a cute,

fluffy, sentient being to be ripped apart by dogs is an emotive issue, because if you don't feel a visceral disgust and revulsion at the idea then you're obviously as bereft of basic humanity as a Tory MP. It's an obscenity which has no place in any society. I don't care that it's a long-established tradition and an ancient part of English culture — so were misogyny, hanging and putting people in jail for being gay. Fox hunting is not culture, torture is not culture. Although I might be prepared to make an exception for Liam Fox.

I respect the views of others in the independence movement, and know that they share the same disgust and revulsion about fox hunting. They just disagree on the tactics and the means of achieving independence. We are after all a national movement and as such we embrace the diverse views of a diverse nation. We are not a monolithic single party united behind a single view on every topic. Diversity is our strength. But on this issue I have to disagree, and was delighted that this time the SNP has put itself on the side of the cute wee fluffy creatures. And not only because anything that angers a reactionary Tory MP is just fine by me.

Some think that it's superior to consider all issues on cold logic, and allowing yourself to be swayed by emotional issues is somehow less valid or less acceptable. But the Vulcans of Star Trek are fictional, and it's equally fictional that humans are rational and logical beings. We're not. We are emotional beings who are capable of logic. So we should start off from what our guts and hearts tell us, and rationalise from there. And the guts of an animal ripped out by a dog tell me that fox hunting is barbaric and wrong.

The argument is being made that voting against fox hunting will goad the Conservatives into bringing in English Votes for English Laws and relegating Scottish MPs to second-class status. But Scotland is already naked and exposed before that risk, and the Conservatives already have all the reasons they require to reduce Scotland's meagre influence. They have already made it very clear that they intend to bring in EVEL — the previous attempt was seen off temporarily not over any principle, but because some Tory backbenchers objected to the method the government was using. They wanted a full debate and a proper vote, not the shoddy back-door attempt to change the constitution using procedural amendments that Cameron was attempting. That's what they objected to, but like other Conservative MPs they're perfectly happy to see Scotland brought down a peg or three. EVEL remains as likely as it ever was.

The most important charge laid at the door of the SNP for this change in policy is that it's hypocritical. However, changing your tactics to suit a changing battlefield isn't hypocrisy: hypocrisy would be claiming that an abstract principle was more important than compassion. All the more so when that abstract principle isn't actually going to result in any substantive difference. The battlefield changed when the Conservatives secured a slim absolute majority and then proceeded to vote down every single amendment to the Scotland Bill, using non-Scottish MPs to force through their watered-down version of an already inadequate devolution bill. English MPs can vote on Scottish laws, but when Scottish MPs return the favour all we hear are the bleats of SNP baaad.

The Unionists can't really complain, although of course that won't stop them. After all they've spent the last few years reminding us that Westminster is the UK parliament and that Scotland is a valued and important part of the UK whose voice is respected. So when we use that voice to tell our fellow Britons that fox hunting is a barbarity which has no place in a modern society then we should be listened to. Anyway, it's not like there's any shortage of barbarities, as can be demonstrated every time a Tory MP — or indeed a Labour leadership candidate — opines about people on benefits.

16 July 2015

Labour's collapse is the end of UK politics

What do you call an Opposition that doesn't oppose? You call it the Labour Party. Labour is to opposition as running away and hiding under a rock is to confrontation. Labour stands up to bullies by holding the bully's jaickit while the speccy kid gets beaten up. Labour defends the rights of workers by siding with management, but then Labour has long since ceased to be the party of the workers. For the last couple of decades Labour has been the party of managing the workers' expectations on behalf of the bosses, but now they can't even be bothered to do that. Now Labour has decided that the best way to oppose the Tories is not to oppose them at all, in the hope that Tory voters will take pity on them and elect them the next time round, which puts them in the position of seeking pity on the basis of being pitiless. Vote for us, we have nothing to offer except malice.

Labour is a party that thinks being a loyal Opposition means being obedient and compliant. Thon wummin in *Fifty Shades of Grey* stood up for herself more than Labour stands for anything. When Labour demands that the SNP set out how it's going to oppose the Tories it's because they've not got the slightest intention of doing it themselves. The last remnants of the Labour supporting press in Scotland publish anguished editorials bewailing that Labour voters in Scotland find that the party is making political decisions on the basis of English priorities. It was ever thus. Oh if only there had been some way of avoiding that ever happening, eh? As a thousand Scottish grannies would say to those tortured leader writers — Hell slap it intae ye son.

If this sorry excuse for a Labour Party was opposing apartheid, they'd lock some poor people in a garden shed for twenty-six years in solidarity with Nelson Mandela. Andy Burnham would appear on the telly fluttering his eyelashes and assure the interviewer that poor people can get by perfectly well on a diet of creosote and old paint, but Labour is the party of striving hard-working families with two nice cars, two foreign holidays a year and a pony for the teenage daughter. Families like Andy's. Labour doesn't want to represent working-class people because they appear in those horrid documentaries on Channel 5.

It's so bad for Labour that they don't even sit for anything, never mind stand, which is why the SNP were able to blag their seats and take over the Opposition benches. It was first-class trolling by the real Opposition at Westminster. It's the SNP which talks like an Opposition, walks like an Opposition and votes like an Opposition. Labour is nowhere to be seen — they can't even be bothered to turn up and vote, although they can and do complain that SNP MPs have taken their seats. Now you know what are the real priorities of a Labour MP.

And then Scotland's sole Labour MP had the cheek to insist to a BBC interviewer that the party opposed the Tory policies that they abstained from voting on. They can do that safe in the knowledge that they won't be challenged live on air. Labour is not so much a political party any more, more an ongoing nervous breakdown, and BBC Scotland is its enabler. But the walls of misinformation are breaking down, on the Internet and in books like this one.

Labour have decided that if they can't be the government they're not going to roll over and become an Opposition, because that's what the Tories would expect them to do. Instead they've morphed into a granny party — appropriately enough since it's only elderly grannies that still vote for them — they don't want to make a fuss.

Perhaps if they help the Tories to be really nasty then voters in England will remember just how nasty the Tories are and realise that Labour can be every bit as nasty. Then they might get elected again. It's a faint hope but in the absence of anything approaching principles it's all they've got. They've been forced into this strategy because unfortunately they don't have any balls they can take home, not since Ed lost his seat, so they're going to pretend to oppose while not actually opposing at all, if that's alright with George Osborne.

Labour has got a disease which gives them delusions of adequacy, cognitive dissonance, the inability to accept responsibility, the loss of the spinal column, and the manic repetition of the phrase "SNP bad".

Called gonorrhoea lectus, they contracted it after they were screwed by the voters.

The party hierarchy is now in full-scale panic mode because Jeremy Corbyn looks as though he is ahead in the leadership election. This wasn't supposed to happen. Jeremy was to stand in order to let the party's left think that there was actually still a left left to Labour. He wasn't supposed to win. Speaking on *Newsnight*, John McTernan said it would be an utter disaster for the party. And John ought to know. John has a well-deserved reputation for political wizardry: every Labour Party he's touched has turned to dust — and not the sparkly fairy kind either. He managed it in Australia, he managed it in Scotland. So the best advice for the Labour Party today is to listen very carefully to what John has to advise, to take his counsel on board, and then to do the exact opposite. Just ask Jim Murphy.

Labour's hierarchy is already spinning frantically against a Corbyn victory, warning that Labour is not a protest party. But if something scares the plastic Burnhamites and Kendalloids and Cooperites of this world, determined to run a country on the basis of a focus group in Croydon, then that's got to be a good thing. Tony Blair has been warning against it — God forbid that Labour might elect a leader who would bring in Labour policies.

In the unlikely event that Labour does manage to unite behind a Corbyn leadership, that could pose a serious challenge to the dominance of the SNP in Scotland — but the price of a Scottish recovery would be crucifixion by the right-wing press in

England. The reality is that there is nothing Labour can do to restore its appeal both north and south of the Border. The malaise of Labour is the fag end of British politics. We're in the end times for the Union.

23 July 2015

Poor Labour, so useless they can't even win their own election

You can't help but feel a tiny wee bit sorry for the Labour Party leadership, it can't even win an election that it's organised for itself. Worse than that, it's incapable of deciding what it would like to do with itself even if it did win, and it doesn't have the slightest notion of how to restore the party's battered credibility except by hoping that voters will confuse them for a version of the Tories without George Osborne. But they still plan to keep Osborne's policies.

Sadly for Labour, Andy Burnham in Thatcher drag isn't going to attract many voters back. Not even Eddie Izzard could pull that one off. Labour these days is as distraught as a woman who's just discovered she's got the same taste in bras as Lord Sewel, and is held in even greater contempt than dentists from Middle America who shoot lions for fun. At least the dentist has a trophy to show for the public odium and derision being heaped on his head like a ton of lion dung; all Labour's got is a tombstone's worth of asinine pledges that were crushed to make gravel.

Labour's bunch of ill-fitting snapped elastics are where they are because they've assumed that the UK's first-past-the-post election system would assure them Buggin's turn in power every other election.

But that's no longer such a certainty. For decades, the Labour Party leadership took traditional Labour voters for granted. In Scotland, voters repaid them for their contempt by returning it dead in a bucket with a yellow SNP glacé cherry on top, and that translated into an SNP victory so massive and crushing that Labour may never be able to escape from beneath the rock it's now hiding under.

However there was another electorate even more loyal and long-suffering than voters in Scotland, and that was Labour's rank and file. They were the poor saps who traipsed round doors, who stuffed envelopes, and who attended boring lifeless meetings so that the equally boring lifeless drones who'd sooked all vitality from the Labour movement might continue with their careerism. The lifeless drones thought that this electorate was so tame and easily led that they changed the leadership contest rules in order to reduce the influence of the unions, thinking that this would ensure that lifeless dronery would dominate the party forever. Lifeless drones are for life — this is the only principle that Labour's got left.

It often happens in the history of evolution that a successful adaptation which allowed a creature to dominate its ecosystem becomes the cause of its extinction when conditions change, then an old strength becomes a fatal weakness. Blair's adoption of Tory clothing was the mutation which allowed Labour to thrive and dominate in the Thatcherite landscape of the nineties. But in the different political ecosystem of the 2010s, the ever rightward triangulation is Labour's downfall. Unless the party makes a radical new adaptation, it's as doomed as Walter Palmer's career in dentistry, and will be an even less attractive prospect than a root canal with no anaesthetic. This will be the epitaph of the Labour Party, that its leadership's machinations have all turned round and destroyed them.

Labour's triangulation designed to lock out the Tories destroyed the party's purpose in the end. The devolution settlement designed to shut the SNP out of power forever has left Labour lost and homeless in the land it once called home. Blair's determination to secure a personal legacy left nothing but bloody broken bodies on the road to Baghdad and calls to prosecute him as a war criminal. Now even the loyal rank and file have had enough. They took a long time getting there, because they believed with more faith than a convert to a new religion, they were more long-suffering than the mother of a junkie whose purse has been robbed yet again. And now they've turned and said enough is enough.

Polls show that the auld left-winger Jeremy Corbyn is ahead in the contest to become the next Labour leader. Conventional wisdom has it that he's unelectable and will ensure that Labour remains in the wilderness for years to come. The drones are apoplectic and some are calling for the election to be halted. If the voters won't give the right result, the right will cancel the vote. The rank and file no longer care. They just want their party back from the Blairite and Brownite automatons who purged the party of passion and soul because they couldn't find a way to privatise it. They're making the calculation that the drones won't be able to wrest power back from the Tories, and even if they do then all they'll support are Tory policies, so effectively there's no real difference. They've figured they may as well have a real Labour Party back even if it's in opposition.

Meanwhile, back in Scotland, the contest for branch office manager trundles on. No one really cares that much, except BBC Scotland, because everyone knows that whether it's Ken or Keez it won't make any difference. Both are opposed to Labour in Scotland becoming a real autonomous Scottish Labour Party, both hum and haw when they're asked about Trident, both are determined to keep blaming the SNP. The same old adaptations, and they don't have a clue how to thrive in the new Scottish political ecology, an ecology that is ever more distinct from the one the party in England is trying but failing to adapt to.

In an interview earlier this week, Ken Macintosh bewailed that Labour had allowed itself to get so obsessed by the SNP that the party didn't talk about itself enough. He then went on to attack the SNP. They just can't help themselves.

The love for Labour is lost. Scotland needs to ask itself whether it can remain a part of a Union which is going to be dominated by the Conservatives for years to come. We're faced with the very real possibility of Prime Minister Osborne, or Prime Minister Boris. Is that what No voters wanted? It's not just the Labour Party that's going to have to ask some very difficult questions of itself.

30 July 2015

Kezitis: It's a compulsion to blame it on the SNP

It's a tale of two tweets, or rather three. Earlier this week when news of Scottish school students' exam results came out, Nicola Sturgeon sent a tweet congratulating the students on their exam results, and that was pretty much that. It was a pleasantry, the sort of thing you expect from a politician. Labour leadership contender Kezia Dugdale sent a tweet congratulating students on their exam success too. Only Kezia's tweet went on to say it was a shame that the Scottish government had made students' lives so much harder. Kezia just can't help herself — she suffers from a compulsive obsessive disorder and is obliged to turn every statement into a political attack on the SNP. She blames the SNP's mismanagement of NHS Scotland for that.

A card from Kezia must be a joy if you're misfortunate enough to be one of her friends or relatives. Congratulations on your engagement, it's just a shame that fifty per cent of marriages end in bitter divorce thanks to the SNP. I'm so happy you're having a baby, labour pains last three times as long thanks to the SNP. Merry Christmas! What a pity that Santa won't be visiting you because of the division amongst elves caused by the SNP. Even when

Kezia is asked to explain Labour policy, she uses the question as a launch pad into yet another attack on the SNP. Kezia talks about the SNP more than the SNP do, and that's quite remarkable considering the party was formerly led by a man who was accused of everything under the sun expect being too shy to do a bit of self-promotion.

The tweet spawned its own hashtag, #TweetLikeKez, and the entire Twitter-using population of Scotland amused itself by sending tweets in the style of Kezia. The Scottish government was condemned and asked to apologise for everything from the extinction of the dinosaurs — the real ones not the Labour ones — to milk going off in the fridge.

Kezia hasn't apologised to the kids because their lives have been made harder by the austerity cuts that her party didn't oppose; it's only what the Scottish government do that's reprehensible in Kezia's universe. Labour's failure to vote against the Tory cuts to the social security safety net, making it more hole than net, didn't warrant an apology to the kids whose families will fall through those holes. It's going to make their lives a whole lot harder, but then they're not the strivey achievey voters in Lab-Con marginals in Middle Englandshire that most of the national Labour leadership candidates want to appeal to, so they can be safely ignored. That didn't stop Kezia demanding that the Scottish government spell out what they were going to do to protect the poor and vulnerable of Scotland from the Tory policies that Kezia's party didn't oppose.

Anyway, even though the SNP are responsible

for all human and inhuman evil, Osborne's budget wasn't the SNP's fault, and if you can't demand that Sturgeon apologise there's no point in turning up for work. This probably explains why during the benefits cuts debate the Labour benches in the House of Commons were occupied by tumbleweed — otherwise known as the Honourable Member for Edinburgh South. This is why Natalie McGarry, the SNP MP for Glasgow East, had the bright idea of occupying the unoccupied benches of the official Opposition. The SNP are the only effective Opposition anywhere in the UK right now. Kezia hasn't apologised for that either.

This is the difference between a politician who understands statecraft and an over-promoted cooncillor. Alicsammin might have been a master of self-promotion, but he'd never have used a congratulatory note to some teenagers as an opportunity to score points off his rivals. There's a time and a place for criticising the Scottish exam system: it's not when congratulating teenagers on their exam success. This is the snide small-mindedness that has driven Labour out of power at Holyrood, that wiped out Labour's Scottish Westminster contingent, and that looks set to keep them out of power for the foreseeable future.

Judging by the media reaction, you'd almost believe that they were hoping for bad results in order to criticise the Scottish government for failing students being failed by the SNP. But that didn't happen. This year Scottish students excelled themselves so instead we had carping that the exams were too easy and the maths exam was too hard and the pass rate had to be reduced. So the exam was too hard but passing it was too easy. The SNP need to explain themselves. This was the lead story on *Reporting Scotland* — not the fact that a record number of Scottish students have been accepted for university this year. It's not just Kezia Dugdale who suffers from Kezitis, the uncontrollable urge to blame the Scottish government and the SNP for all and any failings.

Of course the SNP and the Scottish government should be held to account. Of course they should be criticised when criticism is due, but we have a directionless Opposition which is bereft of any clear idea of what it stands for apart from SNPBAD!, and we have a media which is utterly unrepresentative of the population as a whole. What your average Scottish political commentator defines as centre ground, approximately half the Scottish population would define as outright Tory. And this unrepresentative media is equally prone to screaming SNPBAD! at the slightest provocation. The less the voting public listen to their not-so-sage advice, the louder they scream.

This has now become a serious problem for Scottish democracy. The instinctive reaction of much of the media is to condemn a party which is supported by over half of those who vote, and those voters are increasingly no longer listening to the cries of SNP wolf. In fact the denunciations are having the opposite effect: hundreds of thousands of perfectly reasonable people have switched off, and should there be a really serious reason to criticise the SNP, they're not going to listen. And that will have been the fault of a biased and unrepresentative media and an Opposition party that confuses knee-jerk demands for resignations with effective opposition. Every time they call out SNPBAD!, they're hammering another nail in the coffin of their own credibility.

6 August 2015

Labour's partying like it's 1999

By the end of this week what remains of the Labour Party in Scotland will have a new leader. I'd say what's left, but there's nothing much left about them, and that is precisely what has been their downfall. Whether it's Kezia Dugdale, as seems likely, or that Ken MacWossisname who doesn't even have the highest profile inside his own head, the Labour Party in Scotland is doomed to irrelevance. And no number of shouty wee Gordon Mathesons as backing singers are going to save them. Gordon can't even save himself as leader of Glesca Cooncil.

The result of the contest will be announced on Saturday, and although the winner remains as yet unknown — and if it's Ken he'll still be unknown even after winning — the one thing that's pretty certain is that Labour still won't reveal the exact number of actual votes the candidates got. That would mean the world would know just how many active members there are in the party, and that number is as embarrassingly shrivelled as a male porn star's equipment after an ice bath. Only even less fit for work. There is something that's hard, getting bigger and standing ever more proud though, and that's Jeremy Corbyn's standing in the polls.

The contest for leader of Labour at the UK level

looks increasingly likely to be won by Jeremy Corbyn, who is partying like it's 1999 and all that bleary Blairy unpleasantness never happened. I don't know if you remember the nineties, but it was a time when the Labour Party represented hope and Victoria Beckham was actually a singer of sorts. Or at least she got to pout the words to the chorus in Spice Girls videos. But if you can hope that Victoria can sing, then all things become possible, which is why we looked upon the charlatan Blair and thought he was going to change things. Jeremy is hoping for a Spice Girls revival for Labour, with him in the role of Scary. He's already terrifying the Blairite old guard because he really does threaten to change things.

The current Labour leadership doesn't want Labour to be a party of the labour movement. They want it to be a part of managing the expectations of the labour movement on behalf of the bosses, the banks and the British establishment. That was Blair's winning formula and they planned to rinse and repeat until they'd bleached all the red from British politics. However, ordinary Labour supporters look as though they're going to drag their party back to the left irrespective of the so-called wisdom of the party leaders. For too long the party leaders have treated the party as a vehicle for their own careers, this sense of entitlement is now so ingrained that there is serious talk of a putsch if there's a Corbyn victory.

Jeremy is described as hard left by people who have drifted so far to the right that the ghost of Margaret Thatcher would be scared of them. They've spent the last two decades being Labour's living nightmare, but now they're having nightmares of their own at the prospect of being exorcised. Blair was the supervillain of Labour, but like all cartoon supervillains he's got a deadly weakness, and in his case it's Corbynite. It's like kryptonite, but with a beard, some socialist principles and a £3 membership card.

Oddly, the right-wing people who shrink before the mighty power of Corbynite are very often the same people who complain that the SNP isn't really left wing. They want the SNP to be left wing because they believe that if Labour is left wing it will be unelectable, and they want the SNP to be unelectable too. The very worst thing you can do in modern British politics is adopt a left-wing position. That is, it's the worst thing you can do for the bosses, the banks and the British establishment. That's why the SNP has done so well simply by being a little bit left wing: it still puts them far to the left of Labour.

Possibly inspired by the Scottish example, many in England look to Jeremy as a saviour from the old politics of austeridespair. They've had enough of foreign wars, nuclear weapons and privatising everything. Labour in England might even get its mojo back. Traditional Labour supporters are highly enthused by the prospect of a Corbyn victory, as are Tories who think that he'll make the party unelectable. Just about everyone wants Jeremy to win; the only people who disagree are members of the Labour establishment like John McTernan — who, of course, did such a fabby job during the general election and should definitely be listened to when he tells us that what Labour really needs is more of his soulless triangulation.

Neither of the two leading candidates for Scottish branch manager are especially thrilled by the leftwards turn that the UK leadership campaign has taken. Kezia recently said that a Corbyn victory risked leaving Labour carping on the sidelines for years, which is exactly where the party in Scotland has been since 2007 so you'd think that if nothing else she'd have plenty experience. Ken claims he's a socialist, it's just that he doesn't like any socialist policies as his style of Labour politics owes a lot more to Jim Murphy. Both Kez and Ken are big fans of keeping nukes on the Clyde. They're the continuity candidates, and will continue to encourage what's left of the party to evaporate away like a wee puddle left by an incontinent pug.

But as sure as Labour won't reveal their true Scottish membership statistics, the moment that Jeremy wins the vote then Kezia or Ken will have a Specsavers moment and will be hailing him as a great visionary in the hope that some of the magic will rub off on them and Labour in Scotland will stop mistaking the dead cat of self-inflicted defeat with the snazzy headgear of electoral victory. The conversion will not be genuine however, and the voters will know it. Dead cats smell bad, and so does Labour in Scotland. There are Jeremy Corbyns in Scotland, it's just that they support independence.

13 August 2015

DWP stories are a lie too far

Politics is, allegedly, the art of the possible. However, if you look to the oeuvre of such high-profile practitioners of the political arts as Iain Duncan Smith or John McTernan, you soon realise that politics isn't the art of the possible at all. It's the art of making things up as you go along. It's the art of self-justification. It's the art of outright lying. Although to be fair, it's wrong to accuse John of outright lying, because in order to lie you must be in touch with some sort of semblance of reality to begin with.

The Department for Work and Pensions is presided over by Iain Duncan Smith, who once claimed that he'd studied at the prestigious University of Perugia. In fact Iain went there on a weekend break, had a nice plate of lying linguine in a sauce of barefaced cheek and went back home to the expensive house his wife's millionaire family bought. It's very easy not to have to face the consequences of your actions when you have an extremely wealthy family which will insulate you from your screw-ups. And Iain's career in politics has been one lying screw-up after another.

Back in 2013, the UK Statistics Authority issued a statement condemning Iain's department for its abuse of statistics after he claimed that eight thousand claimants affected by the benefits cap had moved into work. The very statistics Iain's department had collected showed no such thing. Enraging an accountant takes a special kind of annoying. Iain did the same with his claims of success for the work programme, which was supposed to provide training for the long-term unemployed. Iain just makes shit up, and by the time the correction makes its way into a small paragraph in the inside pages of a Tory newspaper, his lie has already been plastered all over the front of the *Daily Mail* as an example of the successes of vicious right-wingery. Of course, the only thing that Iain is successful at is telling porkie pies.

Iain's relationship to truth and veracity is at best tangential, so when faced with mounting criticism of the inhumane regime of capriciously applied benefits sanctions which take from the mouths of the very poorest, Iain was in desperate need of some sanctioned claimants who would say that their sanctions had been a positive experience. Not for any particular reason of improved public image, mind: the entire country already thinks he's a bastard. It was because in keeping with Iain's benefits regime, cabinet ministers have to produce a certain number of positive media reports, or George Osborne will sanction them. George knows all about painful and humiliating sanctions.

Unsurprisingly, he couldn't find any people who've been starved who think it's a positive thing, although perhaps if he'd looked amongst people following Michelle the Moan's diet plan he might have had some success. He'd have had even more success if he'd trawled some of the more recherché nightclubs, because there at least he'd encounter some masochists who really do enjoy being kicked in the nads, reduced to powerless objects who have to beg, and stripped of their human dignity. Rumour has it there are quite a few of them who are Tory MPs.

Confronted with an absolute absence of any real-life positive outcomes from the Department for Work and Pensions sanctions regime, the DWP just took a leaf out of its lying boss's lying book of lies, and made some up. Jennifer was sanctioned by the DWP and it relieved her of the burden of choosing food for her children's tea; now she saves a fortune by just feeding them what she can find in the bins at the back of Lidl. James was found fit for work after dying of cancer, and now he runs a successful waste consultancy business in Kidderminster with Derek Acorah. Richard was sanctioned for being late for an appointment after his bus was caught in traffic; now he's learned that money is a symbol of materialism and is a more spiritual person who fasts for weeks at a stretch.

But in one important respect, the invented sanctions stories are absolutely spot on. Just like the real sanctions, they have no grounding whatsoever in any objective reality. Caught out in its lie, the DWP hastily claimed that the stories were merely for illustrative purposes. This is obviously a different interpretation of "illustrative" from that used by the rest of us. In the DWP "illustrative" clearly means fictitious self-justifying bull. If they'd caught claimants doing the same thing in their CVs the DWP would have sanctioned them more quickly than Iain Duncan Smith could say Perugia University. Because there's a technical term for what the DWP did, and it's "lying through your lying teeth." Otherwise a claimant could write a CV full of what an employer would have said about how good they were at the job they never got and if the employer had liked them. But surely it must be OK if it was only for illustrative purposes. Iain does it, and no one sanctions him.

There was a time, aeons ago, that a government minister whose department was caught out telling barefaced lies would have had to resign for it. They'd have been slapped down and forced to make a grovelling apology to the House of Commons. That's why cabinet ministers are paid so much more, because they are supposed to be responsible and the buck stops with them. They're supposed to be accountable. But Iain won't receive any sanctions for an action that would have resulted in a benefits claimant being sanctioned. It's only the poor and the weak who have to suffer the consequences, not the rich and the powerful. That's the real lesson of Iain's sanction regime. We are governed by an unaccountable class which doesn't need to bother with trivialities like truth, or even basic human decency. Iain's department is also the department which insists that a raped woman prove that her child is a result of rape or she'll get her benefits capped. And these are the people whose job is to ensure a basic standard of living for all citizens.

These are the reasons why Jeremy Corbyn is attracting such support, why the SNP has crushed all opposition, why the British state is teetering on the verge and may not survive. It doesn't deserve to survive. It's a disgrace to common humanity.

20 August 2015

Stateless broadcaster

Scotland is appallingly poorly served by our state broadcaster, yet any attempt to discuss the devolution of broadcasting is treated by the Unionist parties and the BBC hierarchy as though you've just suggested that Nick Robinson be lightly coated in garam flour and deep-fried in ghee live on the *News at Six*. The idea that Scotland should be permitted to have its own state broadcast media is regarded in certain circles as even less plausible than Iain Duncan Smith stopping the demonisation of people dependent on social security.

The devolution of broadcasting is not only not on the table — despite what David Cameron said in the final days of the referendum campaign, when he promised that everything was up for discussion — it's not even in the studio building. And unlike Elvis, it was never there in the first place. Davie Cameron's blue suede shoes kicked it out of touch before it could ever be discussed.

Suggesting that Scotland just might possibly be better provided for with a national public broadcast channel of its own, subject to the control and oversight of Scottish institutions and accountable to the Scottish public who pay for it, receives a hysterical response from the Unionists. It's nationalist bullying to suggest that a public service might actually be accountable to the public that it services. Poor BBC, being bullied by people with placards protesting peacefully. Although if the BBC really is a helpless victim of bullying by a granny from Methil with a home-made poster and an angry frown, then you do have to wonder just how effective the institution is going to be at standing up for the public against the powerful and the well connected. The claim that the BBC is being bullied by ordinary people protesting peacefully is in itself an admission that the BBC is unfit for purpose.

So opponents of the perfectly sensible proposal for a Scottish national broadcaster have to resort to a variation of the too wee too poor and too stupid argument, telling us that the quality of our television would suffer. The implication being that Scotland couldn't possibly produce any television worth watching. The main problem with this argument is of course that the people making it are responsible for producing Scottish television programmes that are spectacularly dire right now. Scotland 2015 is so rubbish that you could be forgiven for thinking that it was bad on purpose as part of a dastardly plot to make Scottish people lose interest in politics. In no universe is it possible to conceptualise a news and current affairs programme which could possibly be worse.

But undeterred by the evidence staring them in the smug wee smile on a BBC manager's face, they press on — just think of all the quality television we'll lose out on, say the same people who commissioned

Mountain Goats, a sitcom that makes *Terry and June* seem cutting edge and original, only lacking *Terry and June*'s sense of comedy timing, set-ups, pace and indeed jokes. If Scotland had its own broadcaster we'd no longer get all those programmes with Great British in the title and weather maps that make Scotland look smaller than Kent, and that would be a bad thing. And we won't get *Doctor Who* either. Doctor Who is capable of travelling through time: in the blink of an eye he can traverse the uncountable billions of miles across the void of deep space, but he won't be able to cross the Tweed if Scotland gets its own broadcast telly, and not even a sonic screwdriver will bridge the gap. We'll be left defenceless against the Daleks, who are almost as evil in their intent as the SNP.

The point of the Unionist incredulity is to make out that it's utterly unreasonable for Scotland to ask for something that's entirely normal in every other self-governing territory, region or country in this continent. Catalonia, the Basque Country, Friesland, Galicia, the Faroe Islands, Bavaria and each of the other German Länder, the autonomous South Tyrol in Italy, and tiny Gagauzia all have their own public broadcast channels. Catalonia even has its own twenty-four-hour news channel. So if you want to know why pro-independence events in Catalonia attract hundreds of thousands, it's not solely because they have much nicer weather there, it's also in no small measure due to the fact that they have a broadcast media which reports on these events before they take place, and let people know that they're planned.

You may not have heard of Gagauzia. Few people have, which is a pity as the Gagauz are a remarkable people with a fascinating culture. Remember the claim that was made by the Unionist establishment just after the independence referendum, that Scotland would be the most devolviest devolved country in the history of devolving? Well the Gagauz would beg to differ. The Gagauz are 155,000 Orthodox Christian Turkish speakers who live in a corner of Moldova. Moldova is the poorest country in Europe, and the autonomous territory of the Gagauz people is smaller than Ayrshire with fewer people than Aberdeen — and yet it has its own public broadcaster. Gagauzia has its own public broadcaster because it's normal for autonomous or self-governing countries or territories to have their own public broadcasters. It's the position of Scotland which is the anomaly. 155,000 people in the poorest corner of the poorest country in Europe have more rights of self-government than Scotland does.

So while Catalonia has its own news channel, and even Gagauzia keeps its citizens better informed, Scotland gets thirty minutes of *Reporting Scotland* after the "proper news" — otherwise known as the news where we aren't. Our thirty minutes of the news where we are typically consists of five minutes of bashing the Scottish government about NHS waiting lists, five minutes of murder, five minutes of oohing at a cute kitten, and fifteen minutes of the fitba.

The reason for the reluctance to devolve broadcasting is obvious. It's got nothing to do with the broadcast needs of Scotland. It's got nothing to do with ensuring that Scotland's culture and politics are properly aired, disseminated and discussed by the people of Scotland. It's got everything to do with ensuring that the Westminster parliament and the Unionist parties maintain their deathlike grip on the means of communication. Because that's what won them the last independence referendum and without it, they know they won't win the second. The refusal to consider devolution of broadcasting is all about Westminster's interests, not Scotland's.

27 August 2015

Intervening by troll

It's been one of those weeks when Scotland has been trolled by the UK government and the Unionist parties. So pretty much like every other week then. As far as Scotland is concerned, the Unionist parties and the Westminster parliament substituted trolling, rubbing our noses in it, and noising up for responsible government ever since the independence referendum was called. For an even longer time, UK government policy towards Scotland has been far more about getting one up on the SNP and scoring short-term political points in the pages of the UK media than it is about responding to the needs and desires of the Scottish people. That's precisely what is driving the demand for independence, yet they just can't help themselves.

The week began with Gordie Broon telling the Edinburgh Book Festival that it wisnae his fault. Nothing ever is. It was one of Gordie's unprecedented intervening interventions of the sort which he does every intervening week. The Union is in mortal danger, said Gordie as he paced up and down like a demented polar bear in a zoo, because of the Tories. Not because of anything Labour has done you understand. Oh no, because Labour has never ever played the let's get one over the SNP and bugger the voters game.

The Tory plans for English Votes for English Laws will spell the end of the Union within a year, he intervened. Of course what Gordie is mostly concerned about is the status of MPs representing Scottish seats, not Scottish democracy. The real concern of the parliamentary Labour Party's much diminished Scottish contingent is that their gravy train might run into the buffers, but the train was derailed by the electorate in May and there's very little prospect of it ever running again.

But Gordie went on, pacing and intervening, without anyone ever questioning him on what he intervened about last year — things like assuring us that the poor, the elderly and the disabled were much safer in the UK. So how's that working out then? Dropping dead after you've passed a DWP work assessment is now the leading cause of murder in the UK.

The Tories are stoking up dangerous and insidious English nationalism, said the man whose party has spent the past decade demonising a perfectly middle-of-the-road social democratic party which supports Scottish independence, and in the process stoking up dangerous and insidious English nationalism. However it's only reprehensible when Davie Cameron and George Osborne do it, not when Gordie's comrades do it. When the Labour Party does it it's just a bit of banter. Only you're not allowed to call them comrades any more, on account of that making you a Jeremy Corbyn supporter and getting purged.

The Tories have stopped Scotland getting control

of the social security system, intervened Gordie, and that means Scotland can't protect itself from Conservative policies. This sort of thing will lead to the end of civilisation as Gordie knows it, which in his case consists of journalists not questioning him because it means that they won't get invited to his next unprecedented intervention, which is scheduled for the day after Jeremy Corbyn wins the Labour Party leadership.

So how's that vow working out then, asked a member of the audience who didn't need to worry about getting a press pass to Gordie's next intervention. It's been fulfilled, said Gordie, contradicting himself without pausing for breath. That's the quality that makes Gordie a statesman, having the self-awareness of a spanner. A really tiny wee one.

Next up was Donald Trump, intervening from across the Atlantic, the only man in the universe with even less self-awareness than Gordie. Right-wing nutjob opposes independence — now where have we heard that before? Oh yeah from the Tories and most of the Labour Party. Donald is a reality show gone wrong, and all that's missing is for him to have a sex change. One of his Republican competitors compared him to cancer, which was unfair. You can sometimes get rid of cancer.

Donald told the assembled media this week that he'd never heard of such a thing as a country having a second independence referendum, which means that he's never heard of Quebec. But then Donald doesn't do foreign. He wants to change the US motto, *e pluribus unum*, because it's Latin, and that's Mexican. He's going to change it to "we shall overcomb." As the American presidential campaign goes on, Donald reveals himself to be a nasty, ill-tempered, sexist boor, and that's exactly what his supporters like about him. He's like Nigel Farage with worse hair.

And then we had another right-wing nutjob with a dubious haircut: George Osborne came to Faslane in a pair of wellies so he could pre-empt Westminster's decision about renewing Trident. Undeterred by the fact that fifty-six of Scotland's MPs are dead set against renewal, and Ian Murray is against it depending on who he's talking to, George came north to rub our noses in his big missile.

George promised a £500 million investment in extra facilities to make Trident even more efficient at being useless. This is the nearest that the Westminster government offers Scotland in terms of job creation schemes. But the only job creation scheme George is really interested in is his scheming to make the job of prime minister his own. That's far more important than eighty per cent of the Scottish population living in the zone that will be devastated and evacuated in the event of a serious accident at Faslane. Nuclear weapons should be sited somewhere remote, and we are remote from Westminster politicians. Our desire to get rid of nukes is remote from them too. They don't care about Scotland because they don't have to care.

I don't want to live in a country that's remote. I want to live in a country where politicians are kept close at hand, close enough so that their backsides are within kicking distance of my foot. Then perhaps we won't be lumbered with weapons of mass destruction that cost billions and threaten the future of our country, and we won't have to listen to washed-out has-beens' intervening interventions being treated like holy writ.

3 September 2015

Avizandum, the magic word that might make Alistair disappear

This week the papers are full of stories about a public figure who has been clinging on to their seat for years and who goes on and on and on with no prospect of getting rid of them any time soon, even though they're widely regarded as being out of touch and a sponger on public funds. Not even a dose of Imodium will shift them from the throne they occupy without having done anything to deserve it in the first place. A useless and expensive ornament, even a garden gnome better value for money. Every time they appear in public, we get greeted with their glum and unhappy face and we're shot a sour look. Yes, it's Alistair Carmichael, the last Lib Dem standing, the Garden Gnome of Orkney holding on to his crumbling rockery for dear life.

Poor Alistair, no one is going to name a hospital after him, and if he's invited to take a trip on a railway line he'd only get given a one-way ticket. He'd have gotten away with his big fat lie during the election campaign if it wasn't for those pesky Orcadians and their online fundraiser. He'd still be MP for the Northern Isles having stood on his record in office, his plea for assistance to Rona, and his sterling work on behalf of the Tory party in return for a ministerial motor.

Now, however, his legal team have been forced to admit in court that he was indeed a big fat liar, but it was a political big fat lie and so his big fat lie was nothing personal. This makes it all OK then. In the eyes of his legal team, although no one else, Alistair remains a man of impeccable personal character, it's just that his political character is more stained than a Lib Dem party manifesto that's been used as toilet paper and refuses to flush. This being the United Kingdom, that's a positive credit to his political standing. Heaven forbid that the voters might expect their representatives to be honest with them.

Irrespective of how the case turns out, now we can all call Alistair a liar and there's nothing he'll be able to do about it after admitting his dishonesty in open court and giving underhand politics a bad name. Despite possessing a political reputation that's more shredded than a wheat-based cereal in the gob of the Patronising BT Lady, Alistair has every intention of refusing to flush away, not even flushing red with embarrassment. He just keeps bobbing up like an unwelcome reminder of a night you now bitterly regret. The guy you got off with after he told you he had a high-powered job and then you discovered he meant he operated a pressurised hose in a car wash was more honest than the line Alistair spun to get in bed with the electorate of Shetland and Orkney.

The court proceedings were broadcast live on telly. The proceedings were gripping in much the same way as being slowly crushed to death in a vice while someone recites Pi to one million places in Japanese. If ever competitive paint-drying loses its popularity as a spectator sport, the Carmichael legal team will certainly be in with a shot at televisual stardom. In the meantime, *The Jeremy Kyle Show* doesn't have to worry about the competition for lowlife liars who cheat their way into your home. Unfortunately, we were unable to force Alistair to take a lie detector test before the general election.

Alistair's lawyer spent much of Tuesday arguing that Alistair's lie was political, and therefore couldn't be personal, in the process ignoring decades of feminist and gay theory which argue that the personal is political. Your personal attitudes colour and determine your politics, and claiming of a clear distinction between the two is as nonsensical as arguing that Davie Cameron's gilded and privileged background, his Eton education, and his membership of the Bullingdon Club had no influence whatsoever in turning him into an uncaring Tory. Alistair clearly won't be coming to a gay pride march near you any time soon, but that's got nothing to do with his attitudes towards gay people and everything to do with him being too mortified to appear in public.

Alistair's defence rests upon the claim that the job description of a politician is to lie to us. This may be true in practice, and it has a great deal to do with why the public has lost faith in Westminster's political class and why many of us want to replace it with independence, where there's at least half a chance that we'll be able to vent our displeasure on failed politicians in a constructive way. In Westminster failed politicians go on forever: they get seats in the Lords or knighthoods. Sir Danny Alexander knows all about that. However, if Alistair had made it clear to the electorate of the Northern Isles before the general election that his understanding was that if they gave him their votes then they were also giving him carte blanche to lie through his teeth to them, then it's vanishingly unlikely that they'd have voted for him. The fact that a Westminster politician thinks that this kind of sophistry is a solid legal defence — morality went out the window a long time ago — is precisely why this week we saw a second opinion poll showing a majority for independence.

Avizandum, said the judge as the tedious proceedings wound to a close. Avizandum sounds like a magic word uttered by a stage magician just before he makes his assistant disappear. And while it's true that there were plenty of wigs and brightly coloured costumes on display on the bench, there was a distinct shortage of rabbits. Except Alistair, who although he wasn't present was staring like a frightened bunny at the oncoming headlights of public disgrace. The term is legalese and means that we will have to wait a few months longer for the judges to consider their decision and to discover whether Alistair is going to vanish. But even if he does cling on, there are no magic words which will be able to restore the broken Garden Gnome's reputation.

10 September 2015

Protecting your rights at work? How dare you

This week the Tories embarked on a new phase in their assault on working-class people and communities. Not content with demonising the poor and the disabled, the Tories have now turned their fire on those in paid work — at least, those in paid work who aren't company directors. Now it's the turn of trades union members to feel the wrath of the party of the selfish. Trades union members are working people, but working people exist to be controlled and corralled, they're not to be valued and supported.

The legislation which was passed by a slim majority in the Commons this week has the aim of making it all but impossible for a trades union to take industrial action. Only one Scottish MP supported the measures. There are no prizes for guessing which one. The only prize David Mundell has ever won is the stuffed toy with which he's frequently confused.

Two hundred years ago, the early trades unionists were imprisoned for organising themselves and for asserting the fundamental right of workers to withdraw their labour. It's the right to strike and to take industrial action which makes the difference between a free worker and a serf. Without those rights, a worker is no better than a bonded labourer, compelled by law to work even when in the middle of a dispute with their employer. This new law gives the employers all the rights. In the Tory world view it's only employers who are wealth creators, not the workers. Those who deserve protection are those who cream off the wealth, not those who do that actual work to create the wealth in the first place.

It's no exaggeration to say that this latest Tory legislation puts workers' rights back almost two hundred years, and once again reduces us to serfs. The new laws are so draconian that even the leading Conservative David Davis described them as Francoist. This is perhaps unfair to the long deceased Spanish dictator, as he would have balked at the introduction of some of the Department for Work and Pensions money saving schemes on account of the Catholic Church's strong stand against euthanasia for people with disabilities.

This government, which recently described the official Opposition as "a threat to national security", wants trades unions to inform the police two weeks in advance if they intend to campaign on social media. So if a trades union official wants to tweet a photo of a kitten with a slogan saying that cats deserve clean kitty litter every day, they're going to have to clear it with the police first. Or the kitten will have to undergo a fit for work assessment and as we all know, you're more likely to die within a fortnight of passing a fit for work assessment than you are to be murdered. Iain Duncan Smith will be standing beside a canal with a sack. So it's not looking good for the kitten. Nor indeed for the waste of police time. This new legislation means that the Tories are the first government in history to criminalise LOL Kats.

This government gained its majority because it received the votes of a mere 36.9 per cent of those who voted, on a 66 per cent turnout. Just 24.4 per cent of the electorate opted for Davie Cameron's merry band of LOL Kat criminalisers, yet the government is now insisting that a union must receive over 505 of votes cast plus the support of 40 per cent of the eligible voters before a ballot for industrial action can be successful. Unions must also give at least two weeks' notice of industrial action, allowing employers to bring in agency staff — presumably on zero-hours contracts — to fill the gap. The effect of the new law will be to ensure that employers who mistreat their staff are subject to no sanctions at all. The government insists that this is a democratic measure, as it extends to employers the same lack of accountability already enjoyed by politicians.

Even if a ballot for industrial action is successful, the government has now decided that union members on a legal picket must be subjected to the kind of treatment formerly doled out to lepers. Rumour has it that it was only at the very last minute that some members of the Tory cabinet dropped a provision demanding that picketers be branded with the words UNIONIST SCUM on their foreheads, but that was only because they feared it might be mistaken as support for Scottish independence. As a compromise, now picketers only have to wear an armband declaring their leper status and ring a bell while chanting "unclean".

The rights of every sector of society are now being curtailed and attacked by the Conservative government. Every sector except those who are already powerful, privileged and prosperous. If you flog dodgy diet pills and fake tan lotions while contracting out your suppliers to sweatshops in South East Asia, you're a wealth creator to be admired and looked up to. If you're a hard-working nurse, a bus driver or a binman then you need to be controlled, and criminalised if you're audacious enough to protest.

Over the past few weeks, we've learned that you're more likely to die within two weeks of being assessed as fit for work than you are to be murdered. We've witnessed the traumas suffered by refugees fleeing wars and learned that the UK accepts fewer refugees than just about any other country in Europe, even when it was partly due to the actions of British governments that the refugees are fleeing in the first place. We've discovered that government MPs are absent for debates then turn up en masse to vote against amendments to Scottish legislation supported by Scottish MPs. Yet we've to swallow all this without protest, while government ministers refuse to be interviewed and defend and explain their decisions. And now the official Opposition is described by the government as a threat to national security.

There is to be no protest against any of this. There is to be no organising to resist. Welcome to the UK in 2015. The Calton Weavers and the Tolpuddle Martyrs would weep. No wonder the clamour for a second independence referendum refuses to go away. The British state can't be reformed — all that is left is to leave it.

17 September 2015

The world turns

A year ago we had a vision of a future that we were building for ourselves: it shimmered above our heads, so close it could almost be touched. We could feel a new Scotland coming into being, sweeping away the old cringe with a new confidence. It was a beautiful time to be alive, as we laughed and danced our way to independence. I felt connected to that beauty, and part of that hope, even as I mourned the death of my beloved partner Andy, who had died of vascular dementia just a few days before that momentous vote.

It was because of Andy that I started to write. Trapped indoors as a carer, the events of the referendum were passing me by — the world was passing me by as it does to so many carers trapped by responsibility. I sought refuge in words that allowed me to feel connected and began to write my blog — the views of a real ordinary carer, not a part of any party or any political organisation, like a wee ginger dug barking from the sidelines. And I discovered I was not alone. A thousand dugs barked that summer.

Over the past year Scotland has been on an incredible journey, a journey that is still not over. I learned a lot from the wonderful people I met along the way, but most of all, I learned to love my country because it is small and harmless and it needs people to look after it. I promised Andy I'd look after it just as I'd looked after him. As I watched Andy die I watched a new Scotland come into being. I fell in love with Andy all those many years ago because he was strong, he was confident, he was self-assured. Those are the qualities I see in the new Scotland that has been born. That's why I never lost hope, and never will.

The referendum campaign was like no other political event this country has ever seen. It was not divisive and frightening — those are the words of a political class which saw its grip on us weaken and slip. The referendum campaign was joyous and giving and unifying. The referendum campaign brought people together who would otherwise never have met. We forged friendships, we created comradeship. We made friends with a whole country.

Scotland beat to a pulse of life as the country reached for change. The hills and the lochs and the streets of the towns and cities sang with hope. We were connected to one another and to the land. We learned to define ourselves and refused to be defined by others. We knew this country could be a place we created for ourselves, that it could be just, that it could be fair, that it could be open and tolerant and inclusive, that it could be what we made of it, that it could be a force for good in the world. Things didn't have to be the way we'd always been told they had to be. And we were doing all this by ourselves, bringing a new nation into being in an act of will while the media screamed naw. We felt their fear and did it anyway.

The euphoria of the independence referendum campaign taught a nation of cynics that it was still possible to aspire to something better. We learned that hope was real, that dreams could dance even under the dreich skies of Scotland. We learned that it was possible to have greater aspirations than the grey managerialism of the Labour Party and we said no to the negativity of the dour pursed lips of those who said we must listen to our betters and obey. We learned that change was only possible if we made it happen ourselves, and we discovered the power of a people in motion. We saw the establishment demonise a nation which dared to imagine the radical notion that a country is best governed by those who live in it. And their hysteria taught us that they were afraid of us — that meant that the real power lay with us. We could feel it coursing in our hands and in our songs and in our words as we chapped on doors and filled the streets.

But as the votes were counted the hopes of a nation came crashing down, overthrown by threats, squandered in scares, snatched out of reach by the joyless. We wept for the loss of the cherished dreams that we had built up so carefully in love and joy. We stood by the shores of the sea-loch and we watched the tide go out, while we braced ourselves for the storms and gales that were about to come. You haven't changed the world, scoffed the naysayers.

We grieved for its loss when hope was snatched away by the forces of fear. But hope didn't die. It paused for breath, it stopped to weep and mourn and heal. And then we stood up. We looked around and said, "No. This is not over." We could not forget the lessons of the referendum campaign. Once a country has learned how to hope it is not going to unlearn it. Once a country has learned how to connect to itself, it's not going to unplug just because the establishment says so. So the dream danced on. It dances yet, whirling, turning, groups and individuals united in Scotland's birl collection.

The storm and gale did come, but it was the storm of righteous indignation. It was the storm of anger that swept away the corrupt and useless Labour Party which had sucked the lifeblood from our dreams and sapped our strength to resist. It was the howling gale of derision that wrecked the Lib Dems and tossed them broken and beached. When the crunch came the Labour and Lib Dem parties stood shoulder to shoulder with the Conservatives. They were asked to put people before power and they chose power, so the people took power away from them. We changed the world after all.

The world turns, the leaves fall, the grass grows on the grave of the Unionist parties in Scotland, unmourned, unlamented. And here we are, one year on, standing by the shore of the sea-loch, unbowed and unafraid, waiting for the tide to return.

The tide is rising.

18 September 2015

Ennobled nags and other farmyard animals

It was said during the independence referendum last year that David Cameron didn't want to be remembered in the history books as the prime minister who lost Scotland. He must be wishing that he had suffered that ignominious fate, which would at least have been a defeat on a political principle. Now he's going to be remembered in the history books for the far more ignominious reason that he was the prime minister who was not able to deny that he got down and dirty with a dead pig, which is a duff bit of pork in a porn scandal. Derision has been heaped on his hapless hamface in the beastliest political scandal since Caligula ennobled his nag. Although to be fair, broken down old nags get ennobled in the UK on a regular basis — a seat in the Lords is the usual reward for a failed politician.

The prime minister is as sick as a pig at the revelations about his alleged pig-sticking behaviour. Speaking at a fundraising meeting, he said that the past few days had been summed up by what his doctor had told him earlier that day when he had to receive an injection. "Just a little prick," said the doc. Which is also what Davie told the pig. The embarrassment could have been far worse however, as large sections of the media have displayed overt concerns over the

sources of the story, something that they never bothered their pretty heads too much about when it came
to stories about Jeremy Corbyn or Nicola Sturgeon.

It's not just pigs — there are also allegations of
drug taking with pigs, although that's not a nice way
to refer to members of the establishment. Davie has
been no enthusiast for liberalising drug laws, despite
it being alleged that he has taken more drugs than
every band which appeared on *Top of the Pops* in
the 1980s. Possibly as a result of their psychotropic
effects, he thought Supertramp was a great band
when everyone knows it's a product of Conservative
housing policy. It's hypocrisy of a snorting kind, but
then drug laws only affect plebs, not those who are
rich and well connected enough to imagine that
going on a blind dates with a pig counts as youthful high spirits. That's the kind of attitude towards
youthful high spirits that you normally only find
amongst the British upper classes and the banjo playing cast members of *Deliverance*. The funniest aspect
of the pig porn prosciutto affair has been assorted
Tory apologists trying to defend the prime minister's
alleged behaviour. There's been no greater example
of public toadyism since Tobovitch Youngovsky told
the *Moscow Gazette* that Catherine the Great's esca-
pade with a horse reflected rather well on the tsarina.

It is said that Davie's descent into disgrace was in
revenge for snubbing a powerful and well-connected
billionaire whose sense of entitlement is even greater
than Davie's own. That's the real scandal here: not
that a billionaire was snubbed, but that billionaires
have reason to believe that because they are ennobled

nags who fund the Tory party with pack bags stuffed full of money, they have a right to buy power in a supposed democracy. The ferocity of the billionaire's reaction to being sidelined is precisely because that's that way that it usually works in the British pigsty. He has reason to feel aggrieved. And so do the rest of us, although for very different reasons.

The events of the past few weeks have confirmed that corruption is endemic in the UK. It is so endemic that it's not even legally recognised as corruption; instead, it's a part of the honours system. Once you get to be one of the pigs walking on two legs in UK animal farm, the defence of your privilege and power becomes the same thing as defence of the state. That's why the government of the UK now describes the leader of the Opposition as a threat to national security. He's a threat to the privilege of ennobled nags and people who think sexual congress with dead farmyard animals counts as hight spirits — but only if you went to an expensive public school. Otherwise it's an episode of *Jerry Springer*.

It is for the same reasons of defence of privilege that an army general can threaten a coup d'état if a democratically elected government downgrades the armed forces below what the generals think the armed forces ought to be. In this general's case, that seems to be an insistence that the UK is perpetually at war somewhere. This is what they mean by punching above our weight: killing people in a foreign land where we have no business being.

The UK has more admirals than it has ships, more generals than regiments, and most of them are like cabinet ministers in that they are products of expensive private schools and scions of the upper middle classes. They're not going to tolerate losing any more of their toys at the behest of the oiks. These are the same folk who told Scotland during the independence referendum that we needed the might of the UK to defend us against threats from outer space, because a civilisation which possesses technology allowing it to navigate the vast gulfs of interstellar space is going to be deterred by a nuclear submarine that can't even manage a successful orbit of the Isle of Skye.

We live in a pigsty which is defended by armed forces whose leaders believe that they have the right to declare war on their own people if the people don't supply the generals with enough wars and nuclear explosives. Yet no action is being taken against a man who doesn't seem to understand what his job is. As a soldier in a democratic state his job is to do what an elected government tells him to do. If he can't grasp that simple fact, he's got no right to his job. But the generals are responsible to men from the same small social group with more money than morals who secured high office with secret rituals on the back of a pig.

The fate of a pig head and a prime minister who is the laughing pork stock of the planet are the least of our worries.

24 September 2015

Come home to Labour

Come home to Labour, said the Shadow Chancellor John McDonnell this week, because after everything, Labour still thinks that it's owed allegiance. That's the arrogance that lost it support in the first place. But even if we overlook the sense of entitlement that drips from his speech like grease from a piece and chips that leaves nasty stains on your trousers, the call is somewhat premature. It's a bit like the management of the Fukushima nuclear plant telling local residents who fled the meltdown that they can come back to their radiation blasted houses because the plant has just appointed a new chief executive who's received glowing reviews in the *Morning Star*.

Labour says it's the only anti-austerity party, in the hope that voters won't notice that in Scotland we have a few anti-austerity parties to choose between. But the truth is that nothing of any substance has changed in the Labour Party in Scotland. Come home to Labour and you'll still find a Tory landlord sitting in your living room, telling you when you should go to bed, setting all the rules of the household, and keeping the TV remote control well out of your reach. The right-wing entryists are still dominant on the benches of the Commons. Labour's house is still toxic, and there's a considerable amount of rebuilding to be done before it's in a fit state for habitation. The party hasn't even started on that work yet, although Kezia Dugdale is already leafing through the B&Q catalogue looking for a wallpaper that will cover up the rubble left by the fight between Jim Murphy and Johann Lamont. That's when she's not practising serial innumeracy and trotting out the same kind of dodgy statistics that the party has become infamous for.

People in Scotland just love being patronised by Westminster politicians who have no clue about Scotland but who suddenly pop up with a great new idea that will solve all our problems. We've heard all this before, and Westminster promises are very cheap indeed, despite all the vows that they've changed. The problem that John McDonnell and Jeremy Corbyn have got is that they're far more interested in the history of socialism in Chile than they are in Scotland, and for their Scottish policies they are relying on advice from the same set of home-wrecking arsonists who burned down Labour's home in the first place. In fact Jezza gave one of them the job of education spokesman. It doesn't matter how good your intentions are — if you're dependent on the people who are the cause of the problems you claim to be solving, you're not going to solve the problems. It's a bit like asking Ronnie Biggs for advice on extradition treaties.

Jeremy claimed this week that Labour is going to win next May's Scottish parliament elections. We've heard this kind of prediction before from Labour politicians, like when Jim Murphy predicted that Labour was going to gain a seat at the general election. Jim's prediction was stunningly accurate: Labour did indeed gain one seat, it's just a shame for them that they lost all the others. Jezza's prediction looks like it's going much the same way, all the more so because the party is going to have a very hard time making his socialist credentials appear credible in Scotland. While Jeremy spent his early political career campaigning against the House of Lords, Labour in Scotland is led by a politician who spent her early political career working for a Lord.

Even if you wanted to, you can't come home when you've got no home left. Labour's problem is that voters are certainly not going to want to return when they've made themselves quite cosy somewhere else. Home is where you make it, and Yes voters have fled from Labour's perfidy and made their homes in the SNP, the Greens, RISE and other pro-independence parties. If UK Labour is serious about attracting these voters back they're going to have to do a whole lot better than repeating the same kind of obvious lies about the Scottish government that Labour in Scotland has been parroting for decades. Just a few days ago Jeremy Corbyn accused the SNP of inventing a time machine and going back to the 1990s to privatise the railways. He's also blaming them for not renationalising the railways even though it was Labour which ensured that this would be a power reserved to Westminster. It's like tying a person's hands behind their back and them demanding that they blow their own nose.

It's already looking very much like a case of here's the new boss, same as the old boss. Perhaps once we have substantial evidence that a party which is in thrall to nuclear warheads has really changed, then the electorate in Scotland will be ready to suck it and see before swallowing, as the pig head said to David Cameron. But we're not anywhere near that Oxford student party just yet, no matter how much apple sauce Labour lubricates itself with.

The signs were not good before this week, and now they're receding into the far distance almost as quickly as a far-off galaxy turned red by the Doppler shift, although to be fair that's easily confused with David Cameron's face as he desperately seeks somewhere to hide his embarrassment. After electing a new leader who's a leading light in CND, the hopes of those of us opposed to Trident were dashed when Labour decided not to debate Trident after all. He's determined to tell us how patriotic he is, although in a resolutely non-nationalist way of course, because British nationalism isn't nationalist at all.

Jezza's speech to the Labour Party conference quickly became notable for alleged plagiarism. His team rushed to Twitter to deny the claims that large sections of the speech had been lifted from a speech submitted to, and rejected by, every previous Labour leader since Neil Kinnock. It was written by people who are a lot cleverer, a spud-like spad said before being forced to admit that they had in fact copied the speech from someone he'd just claimed wasn't so clever after all. Recycling the past in the hope that it turns out differently this time, that's going to be the epitaph for the Labour Party.

For all his promises, Jeremy Corbyn isn't going to

change the Labour Party — he's an aspirin hoping to cure cancer and his new politics are already terminally infected with the old politics he claimed to be replacing. We know how to get real change in Scotland, and it doesn't involve voting for a party that has had over one hundred stalled years on the parliamentary road to socialism and has blown every chance it ever had.

1 October 2015

Tory party conference and wizard wheezing

It's the Tory party conference this week and Manchester looks like it's under occupation by a hostile army. This isn't because of the protests which any scramble of Tories attracts like a clutch of broken eggs; it's because of the police cordons and snipers which are all that stand between the conference delegates and a quiche Lorraine.

The main feature of this year's Tory conference is a contest which none of the participants will admit to taking part in. It's a beauty parade in reverse as various cabinet ministers make a pitch for the leader's job which Davie Cameron is due to vacate sometime during this parliament so he can go and spend more time with his pigs. The country has been confronted by the terrifying sight of George Osborne, Theresa May and Boris Johnston attempting to outdo one another in the zombie politician stakes, making dead political claims walk again. Or lurch, in the case of Boris.

Prominent Tories took it in turns to explain to the country why they've cut the police budget, the fire services budget and the NHS budget, but they're still paying for Trident so that keeps us all safe. We live in the only country in Europe whose food banks and jobcentre sanctionees are protected by nuclear warheads. But we still have plenty to aspire to. According to Jeremy Hunt it's a good thing that tax credits are being taken away from the low-paid because then they can look forward to working like the Chinese: in sweatshops without any rights. Makes you proud to be British, doesn't it?

Boris used his speech to position himself to the left of George Osborne, but since Osborne has positioned himself so far to the right that Caligula would appeal to him to show a bit of moderation and human decency, that's not saying much.

George Osborne used his own speech to channel Bob the Builder, since Davie Cameron already has first dibs on Peppa Pig. George was keen to tell us how much he was building in the Northern Poorhoose, which would mostly be his chances of taking the top job once Davie has porked out. George's message basically boiled down to this: it's a dog-eat-dog world, and we're the biggest dogs so screw the rest of you. As always with Tories, the poor need to be punished with sanctions to motivate them, whereas the rich need to be rewarded with bribes to motivate them. It's a peculiar logic, and by the same logic there must be a median income at which people require neither sanctions nor bribes to be motivated. Perhaps if George could ensure that everyone was paid at that level then Britain might be a state worth staying a part of, but that would be dangerously socialist.

The Tories have already redefined poverty so that they can claim people who go to food banks aren't poor. They've redefined the living wage to mean a wage that it's impossible to live on, and now Theresa May has redefined refugee to mean someone who isn't allowed asylum in the UK.

In a closely fought contest for most odious, the Secretary of State for the Home Office narrowly snatched the prize by lifting her entire speech from the *UKIP Guide to Migration and Demonising Refugees*. She repeated the claim made by the likes of Nigel Farage and the BNP that migrants are coming over here and stealing our jobs, although Theresa and most of the delegates she addressed herself to would be the last people to accept minimum wage work cleaning offices at 5 a.m. Theresa made the claim despite the fact that her own Home Office published figures earlier this year which demonstrated that there is absolutely no evidence to support it. Clearly Theresa doesn't read her own memos. Calling her speech divisive and reactionary would be like calling Sawney Bean a fan of natural cuisine.

Meanwhile in Scotland the Tories are hoping to supplant Labour as the main opposition to the SNP. This is not because Scotland has suddenly decided that George Osborne is at heart a kind and generous soul, or that Theresa May embodies the spirit of compassion. Theresa May is still to compassion as Dale Winton is to cage fighting, and the only reason that George Osborne doesn't take the award for the Man Most Likely to Kick Away a Child's Crutches is because we live in a universe with Iain Duncan Smith in it.

Iain used his speech to conference to remind claimants that if a member of their family had died due to being sanctioned, they'd now have to declare their bedroom as spare for housing benefit purposes. He also called for an end to nastiness in politics. He was followed on to the podium by Vlad the Impaler, who gave an impassioned speech about how tooth-picks are really jaggy.

The Tories could become the official Opposition in Scotland not because of anything positive that they're doing themselves. It's because Labour is drowning in its own confusion, allowing it to be over-taken by a party which is declining into a flag-waving twilight that it determinedly claims not to be nation-alist. Like a vinegar sponge, the Tories are soaking up those bitter-ender Unionists who would stick with the UK even if it meant that the poor become fur-ther impoverished while the rich become ever richer and democracy shrivels and dies. The irony is that those are generally the very same people who criti-cise the SNP for wanting independence at any cost.

Earlier this week it was revealed that the Labour leadership in Transgeordieland has instructed MPs not to mention the name Scotland because that's playing into the SNP's hands. Saying Scotland is a country reminds people that Scotland exists, and that in turn makes people want independence. In fact, what makes people want independence is that the Labour Party comes out with such hauf-baked tripe.

With this kind of competition, all the Tories have to do to overtake Labour is to refrain from killing disa-bled people or having intercourse with pigs, although that is a bit of a tough call for them. However, they've now had the wizard wheeze of bringing forward tax raising responsibilities for Holyrood, allowing Ruthie to promise to cut taxes. As always, the devolution priorities of Westminster parties have got nothing to do with what's good for Scotland, and everything to do with trying to get one over the SNP.

The Tory party conference was an advert for backward-looking and small-minded politics, and an advert for all the reasons Scotland needs to escape from this Union as fast as we can.

8 October 2015